Praise for *How to Be a Rockstar Screenwriter*

"*How to Be a Rockstar Screenwriter* lays out the harsh truth that writing is a profession that often takes years of steady, hard work to get started. But if you're all-in, this book will show you the way (while at the same time being your personal cheerleader). I wrote 25 half-hour spec scripts before I landed my first TV staff job; if I'd had this book at the start, I think it would have happened sooner. Five Stars."

–**Steve Pepoon,** Emmy winner, *The Simpsons*

"A masterpiece for the movie-motivated. With their typical wit and aplomb, the Silvermans have taken the mystery out of getting your screenplay to see the light of day. The text is clear and covers every single thing you'll love and hate about a screenwriting career. Warning: it's not enough to write a screenplay; you have to write a great one and then sell it. David and Rogena are your industry-insider guides to the end goal. Rookies and regulars will find the right path in this book. Essential reading."

–**Cat Delany,** international award-winning playwright

"It should be required in every film class. It'll make the teacher's job a lot easier. Five Stars."

–**Jack Carrerow,** Writer's Guild Member since 1980

"David and Rogena's book gives both aspiring screenwriters and screenwriters who need inspiration the tools to move forward. It puts valuable knowledge only acquired after decades of experience in "the business" out there for everyone to use in an easy-to-follow format."

–**Jo Rafferty,** freelance journalist

"I found the advice in *How to Be a Rockstar Screenwriter* to be extremely helpful, not just from a technical standpoint but also an emotional one. It shows a keen insight into the writer's mind, which benefits those of us constantly seeking to improve. Five stars."

–**Paul Zeidman,** screenwriter

"I wish I could have read this book before I went to film school! Tons of practical, no-nonsense advice from industry pros, with real-life lessons about writing for TV and the movies. Two thumbs up. Highly recommended!"

–**Mark Gunnion,** screenwriter, Founder, Hippie-Dippie Hollywood Hopefuls

"If I'd only had David and Rogena's outstanding guidance at the beginning of my career, I might have had much more success and a lot less angst. Every screenwriter needs this book."

–**Steve Cuden,** co-creator, *Jekyll & Hyde, The Musical*; author, *Beating Hollywood*

"My advice to aspiring writers: Forget film school, save money, and read this book. David and Rogena have written the career guidelines book I wish had existed when I first came to Hollywood. Five stars."

—**Jay Moriarty,** writer/showrunner, *The Jeffersons;* author, *Honky in the House, a Memoir*

"Excellent advice from writers David and Rogena on both the practical aspects of the business and achieving the mental state needed to deal with the fear and self-doubt that all writers face. The perfect gift for the aspiring screenwriter."

—**Howard Bendetson,** writer, *Newhart*

"Sometimes, all it takes is a little confidence for the first step. Industry veterans Silverman and Schuyler's clear instructions are so full of their experience that after reading it, you'll have that confidence necessary to take off. I guarantee it. The straightforward resource appendix by itself is a jewel. Highly recommended."

—**Ken Funsten,** CFA, *Sisters in Crime* Mystery Books, LA Chapter board member

"I've been a professional TV writer for 50 years, and I can say the info and advice in this superbly crafted book are spot on. This is THE invaluable resource for not only beginners but pros who think they know it all. I've found stuff I wish I'd known a long time ago. (Where the hell were you in 1971, Silverman!?) Highly recommended. Six stars! (Not just 5. See? Break barriers!)"

—**Robert Illes,** 2x Emmy winner

How to Be a Rockstar Screenwriter

(or at least pay the bills)

How to Be a
Rockstar Screenwriter

(or at least pay the bills)

Mindset, Tools, and Strategies for a
Successful Screenwriting Career

**DAVID SILVERMAN &
ROGENA D. SCHUYLER**

How to Be a Rockstar Screenwriter (or at least pay the bills)

Copyright © 2025 David Silverman & Rogena D. Schuyler

All rights reserved. No part of this book may be used or reproduced or transmitted in any form or by any means whatsoever, including electronic or mechanical, photocopying, recording, or by any information storage and retrieval system, without the written permission of the publisher. For information, contact hollywoodScriptWriting.com.

This book is not to be used as a substitute for legal advice, psychotherapy, or another counseling program of any nature. If you choose to follow any of the techniques offered in this book, you willingly and knowingly shall bind yourself, the members of your family or those living with you, and anyone impacted by your actions to not hold the authors or those associated with the book as responsible for any and all risks, injuries or damages that may have incurred from your actions and decision to follow any advice, information, or direction provided within the book.

Editor: Mary Rembert
Cover Designer: Zizi Iryaspraha Subiyarta
Interior Designer: Amit Dey—amitdey2528@gmail.com
Production & Publishing Consultant: www.authorpreneurbooks.com

ISBN: 979-8-9925287-0-1 (paperback)
ISBN: 979-8-9925287-1-8 (ebook)

CONTENTS

Chapter 1: You Don't Know What You Don't Know 1

SECTION 1 – WHAT YOU NEED TO KNOW NOW 5

Chapter 2: (Almost) Nobody Sells Their First Script 7

Chapter 3: Zen and the Stages of Writing Growth 11

Chapter 4: Will Hollywood Steal Your Movie? 15

Chapter 5: You've Got to Be "Original but Familiar" 19

Chapter 6: You Can't Write a Script That's "Just OK" 23

Chapter 7: Why You Should Write High-Concept Scripts . . . 27

Chapter 8: Consider Writing with a Partner 31

Chapter 9: Write Like a Low-Budget Film Producer. 37

Chapter 10: Think About Writing for TV. 41

Chapter 11: Create a Unique Voice 45

Chapter 12: What Do You Want to Say?. 49

Chapter 13: Reasons Why You Should Go to Film School . . . 53

Chapter 14: Should You Go to Film School?
　　　　　　The Case Against it 57

SECTION 2 – PRODUCTIVITY HACKS 61

Chapter 15: How to Find Time to Write 63

Chapter 16: How Screenwriters Get into Flow 67

Chapter 17: Create a Perfect Workspace for Writing 71

Chapter 18: Writing Rituals to Boost Productivity. 75

Chapter 19: How to Beat Procrastination 79

Chapter 20: How to Fight Perfectionism 83

Chapter 21: Blocked? Remember Why You Started Writing . . 87

Chapter 22: Fixes for Screenwriting Blocks 91

Chapter 23: Coping with Rejection 97

Chapter 24: How Writers Process the Pain 101

SECTION 3 – BREAKING IN—DAY JOBS 105

Chapter 25: Best Day Jobs for Writers. 107

Chapter 26: Famous Screenwriter's Day Jobs 111

SECTION 4 – BREAKING IN—FOR OLDER WRITERS . . 117

Chapter 27: How Old Is Too Old for Hollywood? 119

Chapter 28: How to Break in as an Older Writer 123

SECTION 5 – CAREER STRATEGIES—GET OUT OF
YOUR COMFORT ZONE 127

Chapter 29: Hang Out with More Successful Writers 129

Chapter 30: Networking Advice for Screenwriters 133

Chapter 31: Best Places to Network 139

Chapter 32: Find a Screenwriting Mentor 143

Contents

SECTION 6 – WHERE DO MOVIE IDEAS COME FROM? 147

Chapter 33: Look for Movie Ideas in the Public Domain . . . 149

Chapter 34: Create a "Mash-up" of Two Stories 153

Chapter 35: Adapting Books and Plays 157

Chapter 36: Adapting Newspaper or Magazine Articles. . . . 161

SECTION 7 – HOW TO SELL YOUR SCREENPLAY 165

Chapter 37: Selling Your First Script 167

Chapter 38: What to Do After Finishing Your First Draft. . . 171

Chapter 39: Ways to Get Your Script Read 175

Chapter 40: Write for the Gatekeepers 181

Chapter 41: How to Get an Agent or a Manager 187

SECTION 8 – SURVIVING HOLLYWOOD 191

Chapter 42: What Is a Writer's Personality?. 193

Chapter 43: Surviving Social Anxiety in Hollywood 197

Chapter 44: Surviving as a Highly Sensitive Writer 201

Chapter 45: Get Your Foot in the Door 205

Next Steps 209

Essential Resources 211

Acknowledgments. 217

About the Authors. 219

CHAPTER 1

You Don't Know What You Don't Know

You may be a novice writer starting out, or you may have broken in and are just starting to carve out a career. Or, you might be halfway through your career and looking to keep it going.

No matter which group you fall into, there are things you don't know about screenwriting, TV writing, and the career choices you will face. The rules for creating a writing career aren't posted. Most novice writers don't even know what questions to ask.

This book will give you answers. You'll learn to become a better writer faster, stay motivated, be more productive, and learn what career moves are right for you.

For some writers, success seems to happen effortlessly. They appear to be overnight successes. Actually, it happens very rarely. If you look closer at most of the overnight successes, you'll see that they were probably struggling for years before getting a break.

They say the average novice screenwriter writes around eight screenplays before breaking in. I've known some TV writers who wrote as many as 60 spec scripts before getting hired on staff.

How do you stay motivated while you're struggling to break in? Then, how do you maintain high levels of motivation once you've broken in?

Breaking into the business is the hardest part. Generally, rookie writers struggle to write on weekends or early mornings before their day job starts. If they don't take classes or get feedback from reliable sources, their learning curve can be steep.

Writing an original screenplay can drag on for months. The first draft is one thing, but the rewrites can go on, too.

In the beginning, you'll be writing "spec" screenplays. Writing on spec means "on speculation." That is, you don't get paid. It can take years before you sell your first screenplay, although some writers do it faster.

Even when screenwriters do sell scripts, they often face ridiculous deadlines and write endless drafts to satisfy producers, directors, and actors. Often, other writers are brought in to rewrite their drafts. With all the struggles and setbacks, how do writers stay motivated?

A great way to stay motivated is to commit to a career as a writer.

Success in screenwriting is about commitment. Don't treat writing as a hobby, or you will definitely lose interest. You should look deep into your heart and ask yourself if you're willing to work the long hours and months it takes to succeed.

If you want to be a professional writer who sells scripts, this needs to be your top priority. If it's down on your list behind creating an internet startup or becoming a lawyer or a professional wrestler, it's probably not going to happen.

You need to make writing your first priority. A lot of great things happen when you make that decision. You don't have to wonder if you really should spend time writing. It's obvious. You need to write. Not just once in a while, but as often as you can.

Committing to anything for a lifetime can feel overwhelming. I advise novice writers to think of it this way: commit to a writing career for the next 10 years. Then, reevaluate.

I did not decide to commit to a writing career until I was 24. As a kid, I always wanted to be funny. I had memorized comedy routines written and performed by my one-time hero, Bill Cosby. When I was away at camp in Boy Scouts, I'd entertain my friends with those routines.

I was obsessed with comics and funny movies. I started writing short stories, then scripts and then made funny short films. One of those scripts got me into the USC Cinema's Professional Writing Program. In that program, I got some real experience writing screenplays with feedback from veteran screenwriters and Hollywood producers.

At some point (probably around my time at USC), I decided I wanted to be a screenwriter. After all, I'd spent a lot of money on film school, so I figured I might as well go through with it.

I worked hard trying to write the best and funniest screenplays I could. Whenever I had free time, I knew I should be writing. When I wasn't writing, I read *The National Lampoon* and studied films like *MASH*, *Lenny*, and *Play It Again, Sam*.

I found writing partners. I wrote with lots of funny people. It was easier to commit with a writing partner. You could talk each other out of quitting. My first writing partner, Steve Sustarsic, and I sold some TV scripts to *Mork and Mindy*, *The Jeffersons*, and *One Day at a Time*. We wrote together for 30 years.

Once you commit to immersing yourself in your craft and writing every day, you'll be on the right track. Visualize it. Stick to it. Commit.

This book is all about adopting the right mindset for success. The way you think about your career will be important. You might be laboring under some misconceptions about screenwriting that will not serve you well.

You'll learn how to be inspired and motivated and how to manage your time. You'll learn how to deal with the emotional aspects of this career, including rejection, burnout, procrastination, struggling with day jobs, and perfectionism. You'll learn the mindset to help you network successfully, even if you're introverted or highly sensitive.

You'll learn how to think like a screenwriter. Where do the best ideas come from? Which ideas do the studios buy, and why? You'll learn how to write for TV. You'll learn how to become a better writer and how to do it faster than everyone else.

You'll learn strategies to develop your individual voice as a writer. You'll learn which ideas are high concept, which you should write, and which you should skip. You'll avoid the pitfalls, and you'll get there faster.

You'll learn about the stages of screenwriting and how to grow through them as quickly as possible. The secret is getting feedback from the right people. You'll learn how to break in, survive, and thrive as a writer in Hollywood.

SECTION 1

WHAT YOU NEED TO KNOW NOW

CHAPTER 2

(Almost) Nobody Sells Their First Script

When you first come to Hollywood to try to make it as a writer, you get all kinds of advice and hear all sorts of stories about how things work. Many of them seem true on the face of them. They get repeated endlessly. Many of these are just not accurate.

To succeed at writing, you need to know the difference between what's really going on and what other people think or what the rumors say. You need a reality check.

If you start with a foundation built on faulty assumptions, you will make mistakes—huge mistakes. You need to get your thinking straight. So, I'd like to clear up the more widespread misconceptions or myths.

The number one myth about screenwriting success: your first screenplay will blow away everybody in town, and you will not only get it produced, but you'll become famous and make millions and can either 1) retire or 2) enjoy a life of luxury forever.

The truth is that 99 percent of the time, this will not happen. It rarely does. Should you get depressed and give up? No.

Even really successful writers don't sell *all* their scripts. Most didn't sell their first, or second, or third. The truth is, your early screenplays are "calling cards." You'll get people to read them; if they're very, very good, some people will be impressed.

Instead of buying your script and producing it on the spot, many other things will happen. One of the best: an agent may be impressed with your work and offer to represent you. More likely, an agent will be impressed and ask for more writing samples.

Either way, this means you really, really scored. Your first script was a huge success. It put you on the map. Whereas you didn't have an agent before, now you do—or at least you have a relationship with an agent.

Another possibility is that a producer will read your script and be impressed. If this producer really likes your work, he may ask you for a "get to know you" meeting. You should consider this a huge success, as well.

At that meeting, he'll ask you questions about the types of scripts you are working on, whether you have other ideas, and whether he could read some other samples.

If you're fortunate, he may ask you to pitch. In the next meeting, or series of meetings, you may even sell him an idea. Then, he'll pay you to develop the concept into an outline, treatment, or even a script.

Some producers have great movie ideas. They are looking for people to write them. If they like your script, they might pitch you a film idea. You might be asked back for another meeting, where you'll pitch out your version of his story. This will be your big break.

Other possibilities: other writers, directors, actors, or friends will read your script and (hopefully) like it. They may

(Almost) Nobody Sells Their First Script

pass it to a friend who has some clout. Or, they may decide they want to be your writing partner. Or they may become allies. These are all good outcomes.

Statistically, here's what will likely happen to your first finished script. People will give you constructive criticism. You'll get good ideas about how to rewrite your "calling card" script. Or you'll learn from the critiques and write a second script that's better than the first.

These are all positive outcomes and best-case scenarios. If you feel that your first script will make you rich and famous, you'll be very disappointed and may give up.

You should get used to the fact that it will probably take a few years to sell a script—maybe more. Keep writing and growing as a writer. That's how it works. You will improve. Along the way, you collect allies—people who respect you and your writing.

Your allies may introduce you to their friends in the industry or more contacts. Building a network of these allies will be essential to your progress. One day, one of your allies will help get you the job that starts your writing career.

If you are fortunate enough to sell your first script, more power to you. It has been known to happen. I hope it happens to you! Just don't expect it.

CHAPTER 3

Zen and the Stages of Writing Growth

How do you learn to write better screenplays? It's a process. It starts with educating yourself about screenwriting, reading books, taking courses, studying screenplays, viewing films, and writing and rewriting scripts. You have to start out knowing that you'll have much to learn and that your first screenplays will be—to a degree—stepping stones.

It's tricky. You have to be really excited about writing your first script. However, you also have to know it most likely won't sell. Remember, it's your calling card. A good calling card script will get you work, even if it doesn't sell.

On the other hand, you have to believe every script you write will sell. No matter what. You have to be really stoked about it. You have to believe it will sell, or you won't do your best work. It might sell, or it might not.

Confused? Sure. It's confusing. However, it's the best way to think about writing your first screenplay. You need to hold all these contradictory elements in your head and keep writing. You have to believe it's a great screenplay. But it most likely won't sell. You'll need to compartmentalize those thoughts when you center yourself to write.

You might not know where to start. At some point, you just have to start writing even though you don't know everything about the process. I remember thinking, "I need to read this one more book on screenwriting before I start." Then it's one more, and so on. I kept putting off actually writing that first screenplay.

Where do you start, then? Read a few books, watch a lot of movies, read some scripts, and take the plunge. Get into the process. At the same time, don't start without basic knowledge of what scripts look like and how stories build.

You'll never know enough about writing screenplays and also probably know too much—in fact, you'll be overwhelmed. The knowledge itself—the theory only, won't get you anywhere. It's the combination of the knowing and the doing—there's a kind of Zen to it.

As your career as a writer unfolds, you'll pass through some "stages." The names of the stages aren't important. However, it's a convenient way of showing how writers grow.

Just as your life develops in stages, you'll start exploring and trying to form skills. As you learn and assimilate those skills, you'll put them to work and hone them. You'll develop your craft. You might get better with each draft. Hopefully, you will.

And as in life, you'll develop an identity along the way. For example, maybe you were the class clown, or the nerd, or the jock. Your writing voice *will* emerge. You'll decide on the genres you like to write. You'll decide on a style. Will you write about dark subjects, funny subjects, or both?

As this process unfolds, you'll develop new skills, read more scripts, and see more films. Most importantly, you'll be getting feedback along the way. How you approach the feedback will be a significant predictor of your success.

Understandably, your first script will be your "baby." You're going to be overprotective. You won't want to hear any criticism—at all. Your first script will likely be the most significant self-motivated creative achievement of your life.

Unfortunately, if you accept that your first script cannot be criticized or judged, you won't get far in this business. People starting out often don't realize they're jumping into a field that's all about judgment.

Your script will be judged by everyone you show your writing to. You've got to get used to this, or you'll have a very short career. But, remember, every writer goes through it.

Like in life, you must adjust, make changes, and adapt. There's a "screenwriting Darwinism" at work. Survival of the fittest. Those who adapt and assimilate new information and skills will move on. That new information may come from a class, a book, or constructive feedback.

To do your best work, you also have to write every script as if it were your best. You've got to pay attention to detail. On some level, you have to believe every script you write will sell. Now, you might point out that I've been somewhat contradictory. First, I say your first script won't sell; then I say you need to write it like it will. Both are correct.

You need to write every script as though it was your best work. Don't do shoddy work on purpose. Confused? It's that gray area. Approach everything you write as your masterpiece, but expect criticism.

Your script may be strong enough to place you in a contest or get you an agent. Those steps are important. They'll set you in the right direction in your career. No matter what happens, don't stop with that first script. Keep writing.

As you continue writing, you'll find yourself maturing. Your scripts will improve unless you fight the process. Assimilate. Adapt. Keep writing. That's your mantra.

That's how it's worked for every writer ever. The pros get judged and criticized like everybody else. Not everything they write will sell. If their scripts sell, rest assured they'll get studio notes, producer notes, etc. They'll have to assimilate and adapt. We all do it.

CHAPTER 4

Will Hollywood Steal Your Movie?

When I first started selling features, I noticed that there was the true story of Pope Joan, the only female Pope. She kept her gender a secret until she gave birth, and suddenly, everyone knew. She was eventually stoned to death on the city streets.

Anyway, it sounded like a great premise for a movie. I pitched it to Universal, but they didn't buy it.

Years went by, but I never had time to write that script. I was too busy with other projects. Much later, I noticed that somebody else was making *Pope Joan*.

Did they steal my idea? Not really. An idea can't be stolen. Ideas can't be copyrighted. But screenplays can. So, I recommend that when you finish the first draft, copyright it with the US Copyright Office. Copyright subsequent drafts, as well. More on how to do this later.

Also, think about this. The Pope Joan story was on the internet. It was in the library. Someone else found the story—just like I did. They thought it'd make a good film—just like

I did. Think about the news, newspapers, magazines, *60 Minutes, 20/20*, and all the other places film ideas come from. Who has access? Everybody.

Will copyright prevent a film like yours from being stolen? Not really. But it can be used in a court of law if you choose to sue a studio for stealing your script. Notice I'm talking about the theft of your writing, not the idea. Nothing protects an idea.

Let's say you send a script out for agents and producers to read. One thing you'll need to know is if you don't have an agent, you'll have to sign a release form. You'll have to agree not to sue the person you've sent it to. You'll release them of any liability.

These kinds of lawsuits are relatively common, so agents and producers won't read a script without a signed release. Nobody wants to get sued in Hollywood. It's time-consuming and expensive.

Do you want to sue a studio? Be careful. Studio executives have huge egos. If you sue them for stealing your script, they can count on millions of dollars worth of legal representation to fend off your $100,000 lawsuit. And if you're just starting out, you probably can't afford the lawyers who could beat the studios in court.

To win one of these lawsuits, you'd have to prove that (pretty much) your entire screenplay was stolen and the offending party had access to your material. Don't forget, your idea isn't protected. You're going to have to prove that a majority of your script—the scenes, the story structure, the tone, the character arcs, and all the other elements of a screenplay—were ripped off.

If Hollywood does steal a story idea, chances are they're going to find different plot twists, change the gender of a character or two, and use all-new dialogue in their rip-off. Consider all the rewrites a typical screenplay goes through. The script will probably keep changing until it's shot.

The other thing to keep in mind is the typical mindset of Hollywood. Writers "borrow" ideas for scenes and stories all the time. Sometimes they call it "paying homage." The *Fast and the Furious* is basically a reworking of the story from *Point Break*. Surfing was the sport in *Point Break*, while car racing was used in *Fast and Furious*. *A Fist Full of Dollars* is said to be "borrowed" from Akira Kurosawa's *Yojimbo*.

Another Kurosawa film, *The Seventh Samurai*, was the blueprint for *The Magnificent Seven*. Even George Lucas talks about borrowing from Kurosawa to create *Star Wars*.

So, there's already a climate of writers and directors "borrowing" scenes and plots from other films, and Tarantino wears it like a badge of honor. However, it's not considered cool to steal from an unproduced screenplay. It's one thing to reference Kurosawa. His reputation will not be sullied by the homage.

If I had to guess, I'd say that more plots are "borrowed" accidentally than on purpose. Executives hear hundreds of pitches and read hundreds of scripts every year. They don't actually steal the ideas. They think they're original.

Don't forget about the effect of the zeitgeist. Call it synchronicity. The ideas are out there. Events like the Vietnam War, 9/11, the Iraq War, and Desert Storm inspired many movies, some of them similar, including *Rambo*, *Platoon*, *Three Kings*, *The Hurt Locker*, and *American Sniper*.

How do you get around this? First, you want to come up with dozens, even hundreds, of great movie ideas. Don't be the writer who writes one script and spends the rest of their life complaining they were robbed.

You can't let the notion that ideas may be borrowed keep you from pitching your best ideas. As I suggested, make sure you have tons of great ideas. Be careful who you share them with. But, if you want to sell a movie, you'll have to get your idea out there. You can't avoid it.

If it helps, remember that this has happened to every screenwriter who has come to Hollywood. The best writers stand out, have lots of ideas, and persevere. They write dozens of scripts, and some of them get produced.

It might even be an ego boost to think about a movie similar to yours in production. It means you're on the right track; you're thinking of ideas that work. Don't get hung up on worrying about idea theft.

Always remember, you are on the same level playing field as every other screenwriter out there. It's not just you. If you're good, you'll succeed regardless. And if you're really, really lucky, you'll never get ripped off.

CHAPTER 5

You've Got to Be "Original but Familiar"

Of course, you want to be original when you're writing your screenplay. But did you know that you can also be "too original?" This sounds counterintuitive—but think again. Consider what's going on in Hollywood.

Think about the prequels, sequels, remakes of older films, remakes of TV shows, and movies based on comic strips. How many *Star Wars* movies are there now? How many *Star Trek* movies? How many *Alien, Terminator, Harry Potter, Lord of the Rings*, and *James Bond* movies?

Hollywood has become very risk-averse in this century. When it comes to business, the Hollywood mind works to minimize risk and maximize profits. Studio executives run this town from a perspective of fear: What if I greenlight this expensive and original film (think Kevin Costner's *Waterworld*)? What if it bombs? What will happen to my career?

The power players in Hollywood are all looking for a no-brainer. How much do you think the next *Star Wars* sequel will make? Maybe a billion dollars worldwide. Executives want to make films that make money.

Consider these three hit film franchises, which involve young adults in a dystopian world: *The Hunger Games*, the *Divergent* series, and the *Maze Runner* series. The protagonists each take it upon themselves to compete or fight for the benefit of others.

Why did these all get the green light? For one thing, *The Hunger Games*, which came first, made a lot of money. The other franchises used the same formula: young adult tries to save the dystopian world.

The screenplays all feature similar elements, but with a twist. The framework is salable, and the differences work.

Another example is looking at all the buddy cop movies that have been greenlit: *Lethal Weapon*, with Danny Glover and Mel Gibson; *Rush Hour*, with Jackie Chan and Chris Tucker; and *The Heat*, with Sandra Bullock and Melissa McCarthy. In each one, the buddy cops have personality differences, don't get along, and come closer as they solve the crime.

Look at how many screenwriters have made fortunes selling scripts that borrowed storylines or other characteristics from successful movies. After you make money for the studios consistently, they'll give you some leeway.

What about filmmakers like Charlie Kaufman (*Being John Malkovich*) or David Lynch (*Wild at Heart*)? They come up with ideas that are almost too original but do well at the box office. Nowhere near the box office of *Star Wars*, of course.

Both those movies are fantastic. If you write stories like that—you'll want to try to sell them to independent filmmakers.

If you're going to sell films that studios want to buy, you're better off sticking to a framework that has a history of making money. Like so many concepts in screenwriting, there is a kind of Zen at play. You have to be able to do two things at the same time. Be original. Be familiar.

This is about selling high-budget movie ideas to the studios. Are there exceptions? Yes. There are no hard and fast rules in Hollywood. However, after studying how the system works, I've noticed that your odds are better if you think about it this way.

If you're shooting your own independent film or entering film festivals, forget all this advice. Throw the rule book out.

CHAPTER 6

You Can't Write a Script That's "Just OK"

"There are so many bad movies out there. I know I could write a better screenplay!" said just about every screenwriter out there. How about you? Have you ever said or thought that after watching a film?

Many writers find motivation after seeing a movie that fails. It may be boring, have huge plot holes, unlikable characters, or hundreds of other possible flaws. The tone of the film might be all over the place. The pace might be too fast or too slow, and the ending too predictable.

If watching bad movies motivates you to write a better screenplay, that's great. However, don't start thinking that you only need to write a film script that's better than a flop. Don't get caught in that trap.

Bad movies get made from great scripts. It happens. A lot of films start as great screenplays. Then, "development" happens.

Once your script is purchased, you will (if you're fortunate) participate in the rewrite process. This is development. You will definitely want to be involved in these rewrites for many reasons.

The most important reason is to protect your vision and the integrity of the material. You don't want to see it watered down or turned into a different film. That does happen.

Another good reason you'll want to stay with the rewrite process is to retain writing credit on the film. You might as well get used to this fact—your script will go through lots of changes.

If your rewrites don't satisfy the studio, they'll almost certainly bring in other writers to take over. With all that rewriting, sometimes you can lose your writing credit. If you're the first writer on a project, you'll most likely get "story by" credit. However, you could lose the "written by" credit.

Sometimes, development executives will give you notes that make sense. Sometimes, they give you notes designed to make your script more like the blockbuster that did fantastic at the box office on Friday. Some are influenced by friends, family members, wives, and girlfriends.

Your job as a writer in development is to make executives happy. You'll need to address as many of their notes as possible. Your goal will be to satisfy everyone who can greenlight your film.

This is where the real skill comes in. Experienced writers will know how to satisfy the executives while not screwing up their script. They know how to be extremely diplomatic in meetings. They can point out why specific ideas may not work. The trick is to do this without offending anybody.

Rookie writers tend to get thrown by suggested changes. They may think about it like this: the studio liked their script enough to buy it. They said they loved it. It comes as a surprise that now they want to change it.

You Can't Write a Script That's "Just OK"

This is one of the significant reasons a film that starts out with an excellent first draft can be watered down or changed entirely, leading to a bad movie.

Even after the development process is over, further script changes can happen. When a director is brought in, he will ask for changes, too. He may want to rewrite your script himself.

Directors are generally in an excellent position to get their way. And they may have a very different vision for your story. It's the same with investors. Anybody who holds power over the production of your script can ask for changes.

This is how an outstanding screenplay can go through a series of rewrites and end up worse than it started. Too many cooks. Next time you say, "I can write better than that," about a mediocre film, keep in mind there are many reasons it could have turned that way. Those reasons may not have anything to do with the quality of the original script.

To reiterate, don't try to write "better than a flop." Screenplays are notoriously hard to sell. Even the good ones. Always compare your screenplays with good films. Strive to reach the level of the best, not the worst. Aim high.

CHAPTER 7

Why You Should Write High-Concept Scripts

"Our main character has agoraphobia, that is, he has a phobia of the outdoors. When he finally gets the courage to go outside for the first time, he crosses the street to a park, sits on a bench, and immediately witnesses a murder. Since he's a witness, the shooter tries to kill him too, but he gets away. Now our hero has something to *really* be afraid of."

That was the pitch for the screenplay *Stepping Out*.

What is a high-concept screenplay? Basically, it's an original movie idea that can be stated simply with a few sentences, has a great hook, and can capture people's attention immediately.

What happens when you come up with a high-concept idea? How can you tell if you actually have one? Well, for one thing, you need a hook. Often, a great hook involves a great "what if?"

For example, my wife, Rogena, and I sold the feature film script *Stepping Out* based on the pitch quoted above. The story had a great hook. DeLaurentis Entertainment Group loved the pitch and paid us to develop and write the screenplay over a six-month period.

What was so great about the idea? It was fresh (at the time). It sounded funny in the pitch. It was a "high concept." Not all scripts have to be high concept. But it really helps if you want to sell it.

As explained above, the main character was an agoraphobic. He had a psychological condition that made him afraid to leave his house. It was a real condition—we did the research.

We started thinking, "What if?" In this case, what if his psychiatrist encourages him to suck it up and walk across the street to the park. Baby steps. So, he does.

When he gets there, he finds a bench and slumps down in exhaustion. At that moment, he witnesses a murder. The killer looks right at him. The killer takes a shot but misses, and the main character escapes.

Now, he's validated his worst fear. He's going to have to leave the house. The police want to protect him since he's a witness. He'll be forced to stay in a series of safe houses throughout New York City to stay one step ahead of the killers.

So, we had a hook. Even better, we thought about making it a buddy comedy, like *48 Hours*. In that movie, Eddie Murphy is temporarily freed from jail to help solve a crime with a redneck cop, played by Nick Nolte. They were opposites, generally a good fit for a buddy action-comedy.

We had the idea that a street-smart and fearless female cop would be assigned to protect our hero at a series of safe houses. Since the killers were just a step behind, our poor, frightened witness would have to keep up with her as they were chased through the city streets. In the process, he would start to overcome his fears.

Why You Should Write High-Concept Scripts

When we pitched this idea to our friends, we knew it was really good because they could easily see the plot and the way the characters changed through conflict. Also, they got excited about the idea, offered suggestions, and talked about actors who would be good for the lead.

Okay, so that's how you know you have a great movie idea. Think about it; is it high-concept? Meaning, does it feel exciting? Does it suggest lots of possibilities? Do the characters drive the story? Can people visualize the story based on your pitch? And most importantly, does it have a hook?

Now you know what to do. Come up with a great, high-concept story idea. Studios love high-concept stories. They pitch well.

Examples of high concept movies:

> *Splash*—What if a man fell in love with a mermaid?
>
> *Groundhog Day*—What if a reporter lived the same day over and over?
>
> *Ted*—What if a man's childhood teddy bear could talk—and swear?
>
> *Jurassic Park*—What if dinosaurs could be created from ancient DNA, and you could charge people to see them? What could possibly go wrong?

A great idea is one thing. A great script is another. The idea alone didn't sell *Stepping Out*. The way we fleshed out the story, broke it into acts, and pitched the character growth all contributed to the sale.

Remember all the other aspects of a great screenplay: it has to have a great hook and a terrific first ten pages, the characters have to be original, interesting, and likable, and the story has to be innovative and exciting.

What else makes a script great? Your scene construction, dialogue, the pace of the script, the character arcs, and the structure need to be strong. You also want to avoid clichés. You want a satisfying and surprising resolution.

That's just a brief checklist of what studios are looking for. Yes, everybody likes a great idea. Make sure the rest of the script lives up to the great idea.

CHAPTER 8

Consider Writing with a Partner

What's so great about writing with a partner? Obviously, there are two of you. You can brainstorm together. You can write together. You can pitch together. Rejection is easier to handle. You can both network. You'll have two voices to to pitch ideas in the writer's room.

Agents and managers like to sign writing teams. They're easier to sell—especially in TV, where the pace is so fast. An extra writer in the room can help in a crunch. An extra pair of eyes can help sort out script problems. A new voice in the room means more story ideas and more joke pitches.

Another reason to write with a partner is that writing is an isolating business. It's you and the keyboard. With a partner, that changes. You have someone to talk with. There's another person in the room to get you back on track when you lose perspective. You can cheer each other up. Spur each other on.

However, finding the right partner is not easy. What do you look for? First, you both need to have the same career goals: writing TV comedy, TV drama, or comedic or dramatic feature screenplays.

Writing partnerships are like relationships: the more you have in common, the easier it is to get along. You don't want to argue all the time. That takes up valuable time and eventually sucks the soul out of you.

So, how did I meet my writing partners? I met Steve Sustarsic at USC. We broke into the business together and wrote together on and off for 30 years.

I met Howard Bendetson in a writing class at the Sherwood Oaks Experimental Film College. Steve and I worked with him on *The Jeffersons*, *Alice*, *Newhart*, and *ALF*. Howard and I co-created the NBC animated comedy *Space Cats*. ("They're furry, they're friendly, they're housebroken.")

Steve Sustarsic and I met Steve Pepoon on the writing staff at *ALF*. The two Steves and I worked on *The Jackie Thomas Show* and *Tom*. The three of us got a development deal at FOX Studios, working as a team, where we created *The Wild Thornberrys*, *Cleghorne!*, and *Secret Service Guy*.

I've already mentioned that my wife, Rogena Schuyler, and I sold the feature screenplay *Stepping Out* to De Laurentiis. We also sold an animated pilot for comedian Bob "Bobcat" Goldthwait called *Bobcat*. Rogena and I also wrote episodes of *Spacecats* and *Alice's Adventures in Wonderland*. I'd have to say, in addition to those scripts, she pretty much helped me with everything I ever wrote.

All of these writing partners have abided by a simple rule: if either one of us disliked a scene, story, character, or dialogue, we brainstormed until we found something we both liked.

It's not an easy rule to abide by. We all think our ideas are the best, and we tend to be defensive when criticized.

Consider Writing with a Partner

So, you want a partner who can be diplomatic. You want a partner who can be thoughtful, flexible, and reasonable. And it helps if you actually like each other because you are going to be spending long, long hours together.

You need to trust each other. If I couldn't come up with a story idea, I knew if we talked about it, the two of us could, or my partner could. Same thing with jokes. I always knew they could find a better line, or we could find one together.

You want a partner who has the same taste as you. You don't want to be coming up with terrific stories that your partner doesn't understand. You both need to be able to look at different versions of the same scene and agree that one part is better than another part. You want a partner who can recognize why one joke or line of dialogue is better than another.

Regardless of how well you get along, you'll inevitably hit some bumps in the road. For example, during a writers' strike, my partner, Steve Sustarsic, started writing for an animated show and loved the hours. Plus, he won an Emmy.

He thought he was in heaven. He didn't want to return to the long hours of a half-hour prime-time comedy. At *Winnie the Pooh*, he got off at five o'clock. He didn't want to leave animation.

We got over that, but it took time. On my own, I sold some episodes for us to write together. That was fun, and it worked. Another time, I sold a feature and took six months off to write it. That was hard to get over, too. That we did get over it says a lot about our ability to compromise.

We finally agreed that each writer could pursue his own projects, and unless something took off, we'd continue working together. Fortunately, we found lots of work on half-hour comedies for years to come.

One more thing about the business side of writing. At least in TV, there's a trend toward diversity in hiring staff writers. There may be an advantage to being part of a team made up of a male and a female or writers of different ethnic or racial origins.

Additionally, if you find a writer with a unique skill set relevant to a television show (a former lawyer or doctor, for example), that can really help you get hired as well.

Another smart move to get into comedy shows is to find a standup comic to team up with. Comedies are generally room-written, so having standup comedians in the room can be a massive plus for the writing staff.

When writers decide to partner up, they need to agree on their process. How will they write so they both get input? Some teams do it together, breaking the story, writing the outline, writing the script, and polishing it together in the same room.

Some teams split the work in various ways. One member can write Act One, the other Act Two, and then switch and rewrite each other's work. This way, each writer gets a pass at rewriting their partner's work, which is fair and generally improves the quality of the script.

In many partnerships, one partner has strengths that the other doesn't. For example, one writer might be good at story and the other at jokes, or one might be good with visuals and the other at structure or dialogue. One might be better at pitching to studio executives.

However, both members of the writing team need to be able to compromise and agree on their final product. Otherwise, the partnership won't work.

If you absolutely can't make the partnership work, maybe it's not for you. Writing alone does offer several distinct advantages. You can write whenever you want, you don't have to explain, you'll have nobody to argue with, and you'll see your unique personal vision fulfilled.

And, perhaps most importantly, when you get a job, you'll make twice as much money as you would as part of a team.

Think about it, and if you decide to try writing with a partner, choose wisely. Writing with someone you don't get along with can be the worst experience ever.

CHAPTER 9

Write Like a Low-Budget Film Producer

One of the best ways to break into screenwriting is to write a low-budget feature. Your odds of selling go way up. More low-budget films are being made these days. What is low budget? Well, there's low budget and ultra-low budget. Let's say low budget means less than $2 million. Let's say ultra-low budget means under $500,000.

How do you know what the budget of a script you're writing is? One rule of thumb is to look at cast and locations. If you have one or two central locations and under a dozen cast members, you're probably in the right neighborhood.

You could get away with three or four locations as long as they were just rooms or homes. Shooting in one house using various rooms, porches, and yards will do nicely.

One thing that helps in the low-budget world is the ability to write good dialogue. Dialogue is free, while special effects cost money. If you're a playwright, you will have an advantage here. If you can write compelling arguments or comedic dialogue, it will serve you well.

Of all genres, low-budget horror does particularly well with fewer locations.

Look at *Saw*, with its evil clown daring his prisoners to do unspeakable tasks to escape. Consider *Paranormal Activity*, where the heroes are stuck inside a home filled with frightening surprises. In *10 Cloverfield Lane*, our heroes are held prisoner inside a bomb shelter as the world is destroyed outside.

Many other genres can work in one central location. Consider *My Dinner With Andre, Talk Radio, Streetcar Named Desire, Cube, Clerks, The Breakfast Club, Hard Candy, Deathtrap,* and *Sleuth*. Notice these movies cross many genres.

I recommend watching as many of these films as possible before writing your low-budget script. Get a feel for how much they accomplished with so little in those films. Some are more contained than others.

Let's take a look at the movie *Buried*.

The film was written by Chris Sparling, directed by Rodrigo Cortez, and starred Ryan Reynolds. Reynold's character is buried alive inside a coffin for most of the film. This script was challenging to write because the film takes place almost exclusively inside a coffin.

That's right, the film opens in blackness, then slowly reveals Ryan Reynolds stuck in this coffin. The camera rarely leaves the inside of this buried coffin. Dynamic tension is created through conversations with others, strictly over a cell phone. The camera never carries both sides.

Here is the set up to the movie: Ryan Reynolds plays Paul Conroy, a truck driver who decides to take a job driving trucks in Iraq. Turns out that driving trucks in a war zone pays exceptionally well.

Reynolds plays a married civilian who has an affair with a co-worker named Pamela. They've been working together for months. At some point, Paul's convoy is attacked by hostile Iraqis. He's taken hostage. However, we don't see any of that—it's all backstory.

What we see is he wakes up buried in a coffin. He has been given a lighter, a cell phone, some glow sticks, some alcohol, and a note.

Paul wakes up to find the phone and immediately calls his truck company, his family in the States, 911, and the FBI. He asks for help, but none is forthcoming.

There is one phone number programmed into the phone. Paul calls it, and his Iraqi captor answers and demands $5 million by 9 p.m., or he'll be left to die.

More plot twists without leaving the coffin.

When Paul contacts the authorities, they tell him, "We don't negotiate with hostages." However, he suspects it's only public posturing, and they will ultimately help him. He has to believe in something.

Later, the Iraqi captor instructs him to make a ransom video. Paul refuses at first, but finally relents and makes a video on his phone pleading for the ransom. This video goes viral, capturing the attention of the press and the U.S. military.

So, there is posturing and negotiating going on from inside the coffin. The story plays out like a chess game. Paul is running out of time, so he makes more calls. He tries to ensure that his wife will be paid for damages caused by his death.

However, the Army's legal department makes him create a video admitting that he had a prohibited romantic relationship with Pamela, thereby absolving them of all liabilities.

Paul continues calling as his lighter runs out of juice and the oxygen in the coffin runs out. He finally calls his wife and apologizes for taking the job and for his indiscretions.

F-16s start bombing the area, and the coffin opens up, filling with sand. Paul makes some last-ditch calls to find there are military personnel coming to his aid. They have located his coffin.

In the nick of time, the military arrives to dig him out of the sand, only to find it's the wrong coffin—they find the body of a different hostage. Alone in the desert, Paul's coffin fills with sand as he suffocates and dies. A haunting ending to a suspense-filled story, most of it told in the dark inside a wooden box.

Buried was made on a budget of just under $2 million. Chris Sparling originally wrote the script with the intent of shooting it himself for $5,000. The movie made over $21 million worldwide.

The screenplay was voted Best Original Screenplay by the *National Board of Review*. You can find the film on streaming media platforms. Check it out. Think about a contained story you can tell. There are lots of producers and directors who are looking for a great "low-budget" screenplay to kickstart their careers.

CHAPTER 10

Think About Writing for TV

I am biased. While I've written for both TV and film, I prefer the pace of TV. You get to write a script and, possibly, see it produced a week later. You work nine months out of the year. You get time off during breaks.

Should you choose to work in TV and succeed, you'll make a lot of money and work consistently. It's much easier to string together 25 successful years as a TV writer than as a feature film writer.

How do you get a job writing for TV? You write a TV script (or teleplay) "on spec" or "on speculation." If your spec script is good—and by good, I mean exceptional, a showrunner will hire you to work on their writing staff.

What are producers looking for in television spec scripts? They are now looking at a writer's ability to spin a storyline out for two or three seasons. They are looking at spec TV pilots that demonstrate that the writer can create three-dimensional characters and that those characters are driven enough to fuel the desired goal of every show, getting to "100 episodes."

Why the magic number? That's the number of shows, representing five years of 22-episode seasons, that networks like to see before syndicating the shows in reruns. Dick Wolf, Universal, and NBC are still in court fighting over the billions of dollars the *Law and Order* series have earned in syndication.

As a result of thinking about storylines that take place over the life of a series, writers on today's shows are crafting more surprising twists. They can kill off characters if they want. They can almost scrub their original series' premises and reboot.

When writers pitch TV series now, networks want them to prepare a "series bible" or at least present one verbally in the pitch. The bible is basically an outline of story complications, character arcs, and twists five years out. They want to know that your characters can sustain multiple seasons, and they'll want to see the season-ending twists and cliffhangers.

You'll need to write samples that will get you noticed by producers. For many, many years, the best sample script you could write was a "spec script"—a script for an episode that demonstrated a writer's familiarity with the voice and storytelling of an existing show.

There are still reasons to write a spec of an existing show. When choosing the show to write your spec for, I recommend writing for a current Emmy-nominated or hit show, preferably in its second or third year. If you write a first-year show, you run the risk of that show getting canceled. You won't get far with a spec of a show that's off the air.

Because of the millions that can be made in syndication, studios want writers who can run their own shows for years. Hence, the interest in delivering great spec pilots. Spec pilots are a good way to showcase your ability to create new characters.

Think About Writing for TV

An interesting example of a writer getting his first job on TV is the case of Matthew Weiner. As the story goes, he submitted a spec pilot to David Chase, who was impressed and hired him as a staff writer on *The Sopranos*. That pilot was the original pilot for *Mad Men*. Years after his time on *The Sopranos*, Weiner's pilot got him his own show.

I've been advising writers to write a couple (or even several) great spec pilots of different styles. For example, you might want a sample that would appeal to a producer on *Chicago PD* and another that would appeal to a producer on *Better Call Saul*. The more samples you have, the more ways you have to get staffed.

The spec pilot is the preferred writing sample in today's TV landscape. However, I recommend you still write spec episodes of current shows. One reason to do this is that if a producer is on the fence about hiring you, a second sample might get you the job. Another reason is that a lot of TV writing workshops require a spec of an existing show.

These workshops are an excellent way for rookie writers to hone their skills and make contacts; some require a current spec for admission. All the networks have workshops to help promising writers find mentors, gain access to showrunners, learn from studio executives, and get feedback on their scripts from professionals.

Some have writer's rooms where newbies can practice breaking stories on a "writing staff." The ABC workshop offers a significant perk—a $50,000 Fellowship. The CBS program pairs you up with your personal mentor. Some workshops (the NBC Diversity Initiative for Writers and the National Hispanic Media Coalition) offer slots based on diversity—including age, race, ethnicity, and gender.

If you choose a career in TV writing, you'll need to learn two-act structure or three-act structure for comedy half-hours. Hour shows on network television tend to have four-act breaks. Act breaks are not that important on cable or streaming services.

You'll have to watch TV to write TV. You'll have to read lots of television scripts. You can get them online. When you pitch a TV show, you'll want to watch almost every episode they've ever written. You'll need to know what's been done so you don't duplicate it. You'll need to understand the tone of the show and the characters' voices.

If you don't like to watch television, writing for TV is definitely not for you.

CHAPTER 11

Create a Unique Voice

Finding your voice is like looking deep inside yourself and trying to figure out what makes you different from everybody else.

Most writers don't give it a lot of thought. They just keep writing until they develop a voice. It only comes with time and lots and lots of writing. What if writers made more of a persistent effort to find their voice? It could save them months and years of writing their way through to it.

If you wanted to find your unique voice, how would you go about it?

Think about your experiences, preferences, and characteristics that set you apart from others. Think about the most extreme examples. It doesn't help much to describe yourself in bland generalities. You have to skip over the "honest, loyal, like to read, like to play soccer, like to ride roller coasters" stuff.

Instead, look at what makes you different. What sets you apart? In my case, I was always drawn to quirky characters. Some of my favorite films are offbeat comedies. Odd, strange, funny, it's a mix—like a Monty Python movie. I've always liked movies like *Being John Malkovich*, *A*

Clockwork Orange, Groundhog Day, The Discreet Charm of the Bourgeoisie, and *Borat.*

When you combine weird, quirky, and funny, that's what I like best. Think of a movie like *Fargo*, where the array of bad guys included a funny, inept kidnapper (William Macy) and some very profoundly disturbed killers who did things like put bodies through woodchippers.

Notice I discovered these aspects about myself by examining what I liked to read or which movies I found the most interesting. I recommend you make lists of books you like—not the classics, but the ones that are way different. The ones you reread.

My writing partner and I shared this sensibility. Otherwise, our partnership wouldn't have worked. Since we wrote for existing TV comedies for most of our careers, we weren't able to set the tone of every script we wrote. When you write for an existing show, you write from the voice of the show's creator.

However, we tried to find work on shows we liked where the showrunner shared our sensibilities. We were lucky to work with Larry Charles (*Dilbert*), Reno and Osborn (*Duckman, Private Dick*), David Richardson (*Manhattan, AZ*), Matt Stone and Trey Parker (*South Park*), plus the very quirky Pee Wee Herman.

All the screenplays we've written have an edgy, quirky sense of humor. The half-hour comedies we created (*The Wild Thornberrys, Cleghorne, Secret Service Guy,* and *Space Cats*) had offbeat sensibilities too. Add to those the pilot we wrote for *Alice's Adventures in Wonderland.*

After a while, producers found that we wrote edgy, dark comedy and asked us to work on scripts with those traits, including the animated feature *National Lampoon's Politenessman* and a Pee Wee Herman live-action NBC television pilot.

Think about writers like Quentin Tarantino and Aaron Sorkin. You can sometimes tell, just by hearing their dialogue, who wrote it. The Coen brothers are like that, too. And Diablo Cody has a unique sensibility.

Embrace what makes you different. Think about how you say things, the language you use, and your unique visual sense. Give your characters strong attitudes and opinions that you can back up. Find your tone and genre, whether it's dark, edgy, gross, light, family, comedic, acerbic, grandiose, tragic, bighearted, or a combination. Write from your strengths.

When producers are looking for something different and original, your voice will be one of the most critical factors that set you apart from the pack.

CHAPTER 12

What Do You Want to Say?

What do you want to say in your screenplays? Creating your unique voice involves thinking about the themes you want to explore in your scripts.

Think about what's important to you. Art? Money? Relationships? Are you devoted to your job, healing others, running for office, dancing, or even academic fields like anthropology?

What kinds of themes resonate with you? Some writers like to write about political themes. Some write about moral issues. Some prefer darker themes, like seduction and enslavement. Some writers want to satirize the flaws, greed, lies, and idiocy that seem to surround us all.

What pisses you off? Is it pointless, unwinnable wars? Is it self-absorbed celebrities? Guys who go around breaking hearts? Find your anger. Try to infuse that kind of outrage into your script. Most of us will root against people who take and abuse absolute power, corrupt politicians, heartless corporations, and serial killers. Those are excellent subjects for your screenplays.

Let's look at the significant emotions: fear, anger, disgust, contempt, joy, sadness, and surprise. Notice that the majority of emotions are negative. What do you fear? What makes you feel sad or contemptuous?

What comes to mind when you ask yourself about your fears? You might be surprised by some of your answers. Maybe your worst fears involve careless politicians causing nuclear annihilation. *Dr. Strangelove, Fail Safe*, and many other films tap into those fears. The fear of a contagious, deadly virus has spawned many film ideas. After the pandemic, you can bet there will be more.

Lots of scripts have been written about man's inhumanity to man. Think about issues like slavery, human trafficking, and genocide. You can count on getting your audience to react strongly to these topics. You want to give them something to care about.

Take a look inside and find what you really care about. What would you cheer about in a movie? Who would you cheer for? You want your characters to have strong opinions, attitudes, and points of view.

You might as well write characters who agree with your sensibilities. Find a way to get emotionally worked up about your writing. Think of stories and characters that are informed by your sensibilities. Write dialogue that feels like only you could write. Explore subjects that mean something to you.

When you write, think about what sets you apart from everyone else. Remember, you don't want a generic voice. You want to develop your own style.

Sometimes, when I'm writing, I'll think to myself, how can I write this dinner scene or this chase scene in a way I've never seen before? Then, I list the most unique ideas that come to mind. I ask myself what speaks to me, personally, the most.

Think about how your favorite films have taken on serious subjects. Think about *Tootsie* and *Boys Don't Cry*. They both make statements about gender inequality and personal choice. *Erin Brokovich* and *The Verdict* are about correcting social injustices in the courtroom. *The Truman Show* and *The Matrix* depict the world in shallow, fake realities and encourage us to look deeper for meaning.

Some writers explore the same themes over and over. Tarantino writes a lot about avenging social injustice. Think about his films. He writes about avenging the slaveowners in *Django Unchained*. He writes about avenging the Nazis in *Inglourious Basterds*. He writes about avenging the Manson family in *Once Upon a Time in Hollywood*. We respond because we care about those issues, too.

Write about subjects that you have strong feelings about. Put yourself in your character's shoes. Write dialogue the way you feel it. Use your own words. Your writing will feel more authentic.

CHAPTER 13

Reasons Why You Should Go to Film School

George Lucas started at USC Film School in 1967. During his years there, he wrote and directed a film called *Electronic Labyrinth: THX 1138 4EB*, starring Robert Duval and Donald Pleasance. The film won first prize at the 1967/68 National Student Film Festival and was adapted into Lucas's first full-length commercial film, *THX 1138*.

The short thesis film Lucas made at USC Film School directly kick-started his career. Everybody knows him now as the creator of Star Wars. Obviously, going to film school worked out for him.

The cost of studying at USC was a fraction of what it is today. Lucas probably paid about $5,000 per year in tuition. Today, film schools charge upward of $30,000 a year, and that doesn't cover books and living expenses.

So, it's way too expensive unless your parents can afford it, you're some kind of wunderkind YouTube millionaire, or you inherited a fortune in Bitcoin. If that's the case, I say go for it. You're going to get an incredible education. You'll study under real Hollywood professionals. You'll hang out with the best and the brightest minds in film. You'll be glad you met these folks when they're running production companies and hiring writers.

Film schools offer aspiring writers the chance to relocate to Los Angeles or New York, where some of the best film schools are. Being close to studios and producers gives them a significant edge over film schools from other parts of the country.

Most film schools offer writers an opportunity to actually cast and direct films based on their own scripts. Schools like USC, UCLA, and NYU offer access to expensive equipment, cameras, dollies, monitors, steady-cams, generators, and editing software. A lot can be learned by actually watching what happens when a screenplay comes to life with a cast and crew.

If you learn to direct in an MFA film school program, you become a double threat. Screenwriters who can present their work in the form of a short or full-length film have a huge advantage.

A little-known benefit of film schools is that once you've earned a Master of Fine Arts degree in film or screenwriting, you'll be eligible to teach at film schools. After graduating, you'll need to make a living somehow and most likely need to pay off your student debt. Many filmmakers have earned a living teaching film, including Martin Scorsese, who taught right out of college to pay the bills.

Probably the most important advantage of attending film school is access to the professors. At USC, most writing professors were produced, successful screenwriters. Why is this important? Produced screenwriters will give you the best feedback on your scripts.

Reasons Why You Should Go to Film School

There's an academic side to these programs. You'll study film history and film criticism. You'll watch a hundred classic movies. You'll write a hundred papers about them. The downside—it's homework. The upside is if you love film, you won't mind writing those papers.

Not all film schools attract successful screenwriters to their faculty, but these schools definitely do: USC, UCLA, Emerson College, NYU, and Chapman College.

A list of other well-known screenwriters and writer-directors who attended film school includes Steven Spielberg (Long Beach State University), Francis Coppola (UCLA), Spike Lee (NYU), Paul Schrader (UCLA), John Milius (USC), David Ward (USC), Paul Thomas Anderson (NYU), Charlie Kaufman (NYU), and Chris Columbus (NYU).

Ten years after Lucas started film school at USC, I enrolled in USC's Professional Writers program. It was expensive, and it wasn't easy to pay for. During the day, I made money writing script coverage, and at night, I worked as a bartender, sometimes until 2 a.m. Some days, I'd get to sleep at around 2 a.m., then get back up at 6 a.m. the next morning—yes, four hours later—to work Sunday brunch.

Was it worth it? For me, it was. As I mentioned, I met my writing partner in film school. That jump-started our careers. After writing together for a few months, we were invited to pitch TV shows. We sold our first script. It happened that fast. We were working professionals before I could finish my MFA.

CHAPTER 14

Should You Go to Film School? The Case Against it

Should you go to college? Yes. Now, I'm talking about college and getting your BA. I'm not talking about attending a graduate-level program—not just yet.

You should definitely go to college for four years. I don't recommend majoring in film or communications, but minoring in cinema is a good idea. Find a major that can get you hired for a good, high-paying job. Writers need day jobs. You might as well get a job that pays.

A business major is a good strategy (with a minor in writing). Why? You'll be surprised at how much of screenwriting involves selling: selling yourself, selling your skills, selling your ideas, selling your scripts.

Screenwriting requires many skills that you'll hone in college. For example, how to manage your time, look stuff up in the library or online, and present your ideas in front of a group.

You'll learn that persistence is necessary to succeed at a complex four-year goal. You'd be surprised how many screenplays will take years to write or market. You'll learn communication skills, learning skills, people skills, and writing skills. You'll also become familiar with subjects like geography, history, politics, science, and psychology.

Why would that be important? You might want to write about a character who's a lawyer, a doctor, a politician, or a Ph.D. in Molecular Biology. It will help a lot if you have a clue about those subjects.

What about attending film school for a Master of Fine Arts degree? If you can afford the $30,000 plus a year for two or three years, I say go for it. Especially if your parents are paying the bill and you aren't collecting massive student debt.

However, what if you can't afford the tuition or don't like learning in a structured academic environment? You can pass on graduate-level film school and write out in the real world on your own time. Plenty of successful writers took this route.

Lena Dunham created the HBO show *Girls*. She didn't go to film school. Her parents gave her a choice; they'd pay for film school or fund an independent film. She wrote *Tiny Furniture*, an indy film that was very well received and that eventually got her noticed by producers. She gets plenty of work and has sold another show to HBO called *Camping*.

Whether you go to film school or not, you'll have to make things happen by sheer force of will. You'll need to be the kind of person who can soak up knowledge like a sponge, who loves to write, and who can spend eight hours in front of a keyboard. It helps if you love the process.

Will graduating with an MFA in writing help you get a screenwriting job? No. Will it get you an agent or manager? No. What gets you a job, an agent, or a manager is related to the quality of your writing, your work ethic, your networking skills, and, again, most importantly, the quality of your writing.

Your script will be on the same producer's, agent's, or story analyst's desk as everybody else's, and your MFA becomes pretty much irrelevant at that point.

When you decide against film school, you choose to figure it all out yourself. You will be in good company: Ridley Scott (*Blade Runner*), Stanley Kubrick (*A Clockwork Orange*), David Fincher (*Fight Club*), Guy Ritchie (*Snatch*), Christopher Nolan (*Inception*), Kevin Smith (*Clerks*), Peter Jackson (*The Lord of the Rings*), James Cameron (*Titanic*), Woody Allen (*Annie Hall*), and most famously Quentin Tarantino (*Pulp Fiction*).

If you choose to skip film school, you must be a self-starter. You'll need to be an independent thinker. You'll need lots of self-discipline. However, you'll need all those qualities whether you go to film school or not.

SECTION 2

PRODUCTIVITY HACKS

CHAPTER 15

How to Find Time to Write

One of the toughest challenges writers face is finding time to write. Most writers have a day job, and some have spouses and children. You can't ignore your family or your job, but you do have to make time to write.

How do you find the blocks of time you'll need? You're going to have to get organized. Create a schedule and stick with it. You may have to tell your family and friends you can't be reached from 8 a.m. to 2 p.m. They'll try to contact you anyway, so you'll have to be stubborn. You have to protect your writing time.

You have to learn how to say "no" to people.

Not only that, but you want to do it without pissing people off. Your family members will ask you to do errands since "you're going to be home all day." Your friends will ask you to go to lunch, coffee, or a movie. You'll have to make sure they understand your schedule is etched in stone.

You'll also have to create strict boundaries around time-wasting activities. There are many temptations, and many of them are addictive. Some are very addictive, such as Facebook, watching TV, surfing the net, texting, and phone calls.

Try to designate a time for those activities, either one hour in the morning or an hour after the writing is done. During writing hours, let your calls go to voicemail. Turn your email notifications off.

You may have to check your email more often for business reasons. In that case, try to limit phone/internet time to morning, mid-day, and evening. If you don't draw strict boundaries for calls and social media, you can easily waste half your day.

Obviously, you're going to have to make some sacrifices.

Face it; writing is your dream job. It's worth making sacrifices. You might have to pass up some dinners, parties, football games, and poker nights.

You might discover you have blocks of time you never realized you had. For example, when you take your kids to soccer practice, you might have a couple of free hours. Be prepared. Whatever you use for notes, keep it with you. Bring a recorder.

You might need to multi-task. For example, if you take the bus or carpool to work every day, bring your script and make notes. If you can't concentrate on writing in a moving car or bus, designate that time to check emails and phone calls.

Unfortunately, you'll have to cut down on some of your activities. Admit it, though, there are plenty of dinners you won't mind skipping.

Your beloved spouse may be able to help you out here if you're very, very lucky. If you're invited out as a couple to dinner or a party, maybe your partner could go alone and "represent the family." If they help you out this way, be very nice to them. You're going to owe them for the rest of your life.

You've got to prioritize your activities. Break down your to-do list into four categories: Urgent, important, not urgent, and not important. Do the urgent/important stuff first.

Try the "two-minute rule." If it's on your "to-do" list and you can do it in two minutes, don't wait. Just do it. Get it out of the way. It will be over before you know it, and you can quickly return to writing.

Let's look at a typical day in your work life. Let's say you work a 40-hour weekday job. Once you leave the house for work, you'll be tired—you might not be able to write.

One solution, which doesn't sound like much fun but may be necessary, is to wake up an hour and a half earlier every day. Get up, make coffee, and write three pages before work.

If you get a two-week vacation, spend a week with your family, then a week with your screenplay. Someday, when you're a working screenwriter, you'll be happy you found these odd times to write.

You also need to remember to take care of yourself. Take breaks, splash water on your face, get plenty of sleep, exercise, watch movies, read books, spend time with your family, go to church, get massages, go out with your friends and play pool, and do whatever else you do to recharge.

CHAPTER 16

How Screenwriters Get into Flow

Most writers have experienced the "flow state." For me, it happens late at night when there are few distractions and no errands or other tasks to worry about. For others, it occurs in the ungodly early hours, after getting up at 5 a.m.

Some writers call it being "in the zone." Others call it "flow" or being in "a state of flow." It involves feeling relaxed yet productive for a prolonged period while writing. During this period, your ability to concentrate feels heightened. Your confidence is high.

While the focus on the task at hand is sharp, everything else on your mind falls away. You feel completely immersed in your script. Everything comes to you naturally, without too much effort.

Whatever you call it, it's something every writer welcomes but can't always conjure up.

I think it helps to have a pretty good idea about what you're going to write during these periods since you don't want to stop to rethink things during the flow. You might want to have an outline in front of you to keep you on track.

The idea is to prepare, clear your mind, get started, keep moving forward, and let momentum fuel your creativity.

You'll need to avoid distractions. If you're hungry or thirsty, you'll want to head to the refrigerator. If you're tired, grab some coffee. If you're angry, you've got to chill. If you're stressed, calm down.

Try to relax. Use yoga breathing, mindfulness meditation, physical relaxation, music, lighting, or whatever works.

A relaxation ritual that works for a lot of people involves visualization. Picture yourself in a peaceful environment, such as a secluded beach or a mountain cabin. Focus on how it feels to be there.

Concentrate on the sensory stimulus in your visualization. What do you see and hear? Let that inform how you feel in your body and your mind. Hopefully, you'll feel relaxed and energized.

Along with learning to relax, it's essential to dial down your "inner critic" during the writing process. To oversimplify a bit, your inner critic is the combined voice of all the people who've been critical of you throughout your life, often going back to a highly critical parent.

While those critical thoughts are there to keep you doing your best work, they can also take a toll. They can eat away at your self-confidence and slow or stop your train of thought. The idea during the "flow state" is to keep moving forward.

When you catch yourself thinking self-critical thoughts, immediately challenge them. Be aware of them. Expect them. And when you encounter them—stop. Stop thinking about them.

You're going to encounter those thoughts. But you don't have to dwell on them or obsess about them. You can decide to move on.

What if it's tough to stop negative self-talk?

If you're having trouble ignoring self-critical thoughts, you might have to challenge them. If you doubt your abilities, keep an arsenal of challenges ready.

Let's say you've published novels or placed in film festivals or screenwriting contests. Maybe you've made some short films that have earned critical success. Use those facts. Win that imaginary argument. Always challenge negative self-talk.

When I encounter self-doubt while writing, I stop, catch myself, and think, "Wait, I've been writing for 30 years; I created five TV shows. Of course, I can do this." This is not the time to be humble. Remind yourself of your accomplishments. Revisit your wins.

Use these "mind hacks"—or as I sometimes call them "reframes," or just "different ways of thinking" to stop self-critical thought during the flow period. The more you do it, the easier it gets.

Clear your distractions, settle yourself, relax, and focus on the writing. Shake off your to-do list. Make the coffee. Pour the wine. Whatever works. Turn down the lights, turn up the music. Make sure you have a plan, an outline—a beat sheet, take a deep breath, get started, and let the flow carry you as far as it can. Criticism comes later, during the rewrite.

CHAPTER 17

Create a Perfect Workspace for Writing

Where do you like to write? Where do you feel the most comfortable and the least distracted? Do you like it dark and womb-like or open and bright? Do you decorate your office with family photos or movie posters? Where do you do your best work?

Clearly, your mood can vary depending on your surroundings. Generally, writers like a reasonably quiet workspace where they won't be too distracted. If you work best in a clean, organized, uncluttered environment, ensure your workspace reflects that.

There are many screenwriting groups on Facebook and LinkedIn. They're all free if you're interested in joining. One is called *Zero Draft Thirty*, one's called *Hippie-Dippie Hollywood Hopefuls*, and another is *Screenwriters Who Can Actually Write*.

I asked the members about their perfect workspaces. One told me they limit distractions by leaving their cell phones in another room. One liked to work in complete silence. One soundproofed his office. Another had software that kept her from surfing the web.

A couple of writers told me they need coffee and cigarettes. One liked to write on a laptop in the kitchen. Some wanted to work on the kitchen counter. Others said they needed to be close to the refrigerator. Oddly, one said the gentle hum the refrigerator emitted had a soothing effect.

While one writer preferred his office to be uncluttered and quiet, another said he liked loud rock music playing. Some wanted to have the TV on, and some preferred clutter. It made them feel they were getting things done. Some writers liked to pace around, acting out the scenes they wrote.

One writer liked to videotape himself acting out a scene. Another talked the story out with his cat. One said he spoke to his Amazon Alexa, asking her to play smooth jazz or to set a timer when he needed to work faster.

While some writers find it helpful to walk around or talk out their scenes, others find it helps to look at a beautiful view. Several writers said they liked to look out their windows at a body of water. It was a calming influence. One writer liked the view of a lake, another, the Atlantic Ocean.

One of these writers said she had a particular setup for writing horror films. She'd sit in the dark, burning graveyard incense, with only Christmas lights on and dark music playing. Her favorite music for the task was Marilyn Manson or Dead Can Dance.

She liked to call this space her portable altar of death. While it kept her writing, it also freaked her out, and the dark energy that came with it troubled her. After she finished writing, she said she burnt sage and prayed.

Some writers preferred to brainstorm in a specific location, for example, in a rocker, a barber chair, a La-Z-Boy, on the floor, or in the car driving up the coast, stopping to admire the view. They'd text or email themselves the work.

I like to write in longhand first, generally lying on the bed in my bedroom. Then, I'd go back to the office to type it up.

I move around a lot during different stages of the writing process. I always print up the scene and take it somewhere else to pencil in changes—sometimes with the TV on and music blaring. Then, it's back to the keyboard.

I'm unsure why I like to have that wall of sound while I write. It probably has to do with not wanting to feel alone. When I think of it, the combination of the TV talking heads and the loud music makes me feel like I'm working in a bar.

Another thing about the office I like to work in—I like it dark and womb-like, with the fan on and maybe a small window open. I also like to be surrounded by cool stuff. I have some artwork and photos of my family, friends, and my dog. I have an Egyptian stone cat with marbles in her eyes that light up when the fireplace is crackling.

No matter how you've set up your workspace, whether you have the most beautiful antique desk, just the right music, or the perfect ocean view, you still have to actually sit down and write. The environment you set up is like a stage, a container for creative thought. Hopefully, it will inspire you to do your best work.

CHAPTER 18

Writing Rituals to Boost Productivity

I've heard it said that "Eighty percent of success is showing up." It's great advice. Just sitting down at the keyboard is a good ritual to get you started writing every day. I did some research into various rituals famous writers have used to increase productivity. Here are a few that you may find helpful.

Stephen King

During the period when he wrote *Carrie, Cujo, Salem's Lot,* and *Christine*, Stephen King started with a different ritual. He worked from late at night and continued through the morning, fueled by cocaine and a twelve-pack of beer—every night.

Since those days, there have been family interventions, stints in rehab, and recovery. King's current ritual is different: he makes a cup of tea first thing at around 8 a.m. Then, before he sits down to write, he takes vitamins, plays his favorite music, and sits in the same seat, with papers scattered around his desk, the same desk—just so.

Joan Didion

Credits: *A Star Is Born* (screenplay), *The Panic In Needle Park* (screenplay), *Up Close and Personal* (screenplay)

Didion writes during the day, then has dinner and drinks, during which she reviews the pages from that afternoon. She says she needs dinner and a stiff drink to give her space away from the pages. She uses that time in the evening to make notes on her work.

When she starts writing the next day, she knows just where to start—it's easier than facing a blank screen. Once she's on a roll, it's easier for her to move on to new territory.

Jack Kerouac

Credits: *Pull My Daisy* (screenplay), *On the Road* (source material), *Big Sur* (source material).

On the Road was apparently based on Kerouac's travels with Neal Cassady, during which they immersed themselves entirely into a lifestyle of sex, drugs, and jazz. You could say that experience was part of his ritual.

One of Kerouac's rituals involved lighting a candle around midnight, writing by its light, and then blowing it out when he was finished writing, close to dawn. He's quoted as saying he wrote *On the Road* on a single scroll of paper in a week. It's rumored drugs were involved.

Some of his other rituals: When he took breaks, he did headstands, then stayed balanced while bringing his feet down to touch the floor nine times. He would regularly pray to Jesus for his sanity and to take care of his cat, his wife, and his paralyzed mother.

Kurt Vonnegut

Credits: *Slaughterhouse-Five* (source material), *Happy Birthday Wanda June* (screenplay), *Breakfast of Champions* (story by)

Vonnegut wrote about his routine in a letter to his wife, explaining that he starts at 5:30 a.m., waking and writing until 8:30. At that time, he'd break for breakfast and continue writing until 10 a.m.

After he finished writing at 10 a.m., he would walk into town, run errands, swim for a half hour, do push-ups and sit-ups, and then return home at 11:45 a.m.

The rest of his day involved reading and teaching literature. A few belts of Scotch capped off the day. Then, he either went out to bars or listened to jazz until he went to sleep at 10 p.m.

Maya Angelou

Credits: *I Know Why the Caged Bird Sings* (screenplay), *Georgia, Georgia* (screenplay), *Sister, Sister* (teleplay)

Among her peculiar rituals, Angelou kept a hotel room in her hometown and paid for it monthly. At 6:30 a.m., she went to the hotel room to write. She always kept a copy of Roget's Thesaurus and the Bible in the room to provide inspiration or distraction.

She had a theory about the Big Mind and the Little Mind. She could do crossword puzzles, play cards, or read the Bible with the Little Mind while calling on the Big Mind to help her with the more profound subject matter she was writing about.

Angelou had some strict habits regarding the hotel room. The maids were not allowed to clean up in case she lost a page and had to find it later. She always wrote until around 2 p.m., then returned home with the pages to make notes and edit.

Looking at this particular group of screenwriters, some common ritualistic elements are evident:

1. They started writing at the ungodly hour of 5:30 a.m. (Sometimes, it was a slightly more reasonable hour, say 6:30 or 8 a.m. Still—early.)
2. If they didn't start at dawn, they tended to start later in the day (or evening) and run all night long—which is my personal preference.
3. Many of these rituals involved some form of exercise, such as headstands or pushups, but more reasonably—taking walks.
4. Almost all of these writers seemed to integrate drinking alcohol—wine or Scotch—into their routines. For some, it was a break.
5. Some of them indulged in taking various drugs—including cocaine and amphetamines. Aaron Sorkin has also publicly talked about writing with the aid of cocaine.

I don't think it's a big secret that a lot of the writers I talk about in this book used recreational drugs. Some of the showrunners, writers, and stars we worked with smoked pot. No names. That's a different book.

For what it's worth, I certainly don't recommend using illegal drugs to help you write—especially cocaine, for obvious reasons—it's expensive. And, as I mentioned, illegal. Come to think of it, a good Scotch isn't that cheap, either.

CHAPTER 19

How to Beat Procrastination

What happens when you procrastinate? You know you should be writing. You just don't feel like it. You feel kind of guilty about it. That makes it worse. You don't feel good about yourself. And that erodes your confidence. Now, you really don't feel like it. You've come full circle.

Where does it start? You might feel unsure about your writing choices. You might have lost your way in the narrative. You might doubt your story. You just keep putting it off. And the more you do that, the harder it is to start writing again.

If you don't finish your script, you won't have to face the fact that maybe it's just not that good. If you keep putting it off, no one will ever read it. Could that be what procrastination is all about? Fear of being judged? Fear of disappointing yourself?

How do you deal with these fears? During the first draft, you can get away with a "good enough" version. You can even write a "shitty" draft. However, when you write your next few drafts, your script has to get better. What if it gets worse?

Writing, at some level, is all about confidence. How will you create a new world if you don't feel like it's all that good?

Doubts creep in. What if nobody likes it? What if nobody buys it? Have I just wasted all this time?

What if you have these doubts? Ask writers you trust to critique the pages you have written so far. If they love what you've done, you'll find it easier to keep writing. Make sense?

What if you feel good about your screenplay but get stuck?

What if you're too tired or feel like you've hit a brick wall? It might be that you're just tired of the process. Sometimes, it helps to take a short break; otherwise, you're just procrastinating again.

Another way to go. Your "writing muscles" are out of shape, so start writing about anything. You can just write stream of consciousness. Or write a letter to yourself about the script. Write about anything just to get your "mojo" back.

Writing about procrastination can get you back to work.

You could discuss it with another writer. Ask how they get motivated and how they deal with it. This is a universal problem. Every writer handles it their own way. Ask around.

Try using a "virtual deadline." I use this trick—when I sit down to write, I'll give myself two hours to write. During that time, I'll write as though there was a hard deadline. Sometimes, I'll check the clock. Other times, I'll set a timer. I'll write for two straight hours.

Then I'll take a break, usually for a half-hour. During that period, I'll check texts and emails, play a videogame, make calls, or whatever. Then, I'll set another deadline. Another two hours to write, followed by a 30-minute break. And so on. After you finish three sets, you'll have done six hours of work.

When you write to a deadline, you bring your full attention to the task. You get things done quickly, then have time to breathe, as it were, and play during breaks, which keeps your mind sharp.

You need to be accountable. When you work for a studio, your reputation is on the line. Money is riding on the finished script. It has to be great. It has to get done on time. When it's all on the line, you get it done. You have to.

Most screenwriters are working on spec. So, there's nobody setting deadlines. No financial goal. Who's going to hold you accountable?

I suggest getting a writing buddy. It could be another writer in your class, your writer's group, or someone you met networking. You help each other, keep each other accountable, and set deadlines for each other.

When your buddy misses a deadline, talk him through it. Remind him why he moved to LA, turned down that lucrative job offer, and broke up with his girlfriend—all to write screenplays. So, tell him to stop whining and get to work.

More "Mind Hacks"

Remember how good it feels to finish a scene or an act. Focus on getting it done. Reward yourself for completing short-term goals. Have a beer. See a movie.

When you have too many things on your to-do list, try to get the most difficult task done first. The rest will feel more manageable. Let's say you have to balance your checkbook. Get it out of the way early while you have energy.

Sometimes, you get to a point where you're unsure what to do. You can't decide. Don't let this throw you off. Think about the decision as a separate task. Give yourself a deadline to make the decision.

You might think, "I'm just not that interested in writing today." Schedule some time to write when you are at your best. If you're a morning person, start early. If you're a night person, write after midnight.

Remember, every writer gets distracted. Don't beat yourself up when it happens to you.

When you find yourself getting distracted, feeling down, or losing confidence and thinking about giving up, try using some of these strategies. They're meant to get you back on track.

CHAPTER 20

How to Fight Perfectionism

The healthy kind of perfectionism is about doing your best work. That's what we all aspire to. We all want to create the best scripts we possibly can.

The unhealthy perfectionist tends to lose sight of the big picture. They fall prey to self-defeating patterns. They make poor decisions. Writers with this issue tend to obsess over unimportant details or get stuck, endlessly rethinking the same scenes over and over.

These writers usually have a really strong inner critic. Too strong. They're constantly second-guessing themselves. As a result, they're never quite satisfied.

A lot of good scripts have been overwritten in the name of perfectionism. I've done it myself. My issue—I'll spend endless hours punching up the jokes, to the point where I miss story problems.

I know I've been guilty of waiting until the "perfect time" to write. That's a common issue with perfectionists. I would think, "I need a block of six hours to write. I guess I'll have to do it next week." I was just putting it off.

Perfectionism is a habitual way of thinking. Lots of writers fall into these "mind traps" without realizing it.

Here are some practical guidelines that can help you avoid these traps.

- **Don't compare**

When you compare your work with successful writers, you always come up short. It's okay to feel inspired by Tarantino's work. It's another thing to measure your work by his standards. You may get there eventually, but don't be discouraged if you're not there yet.

Don't fall into the trap of thinking in "all or nothing" terms. This thinking goes like this, "If my script isn't perfect, it's a failure. There's nothing in between." There is plenty in between.

Remember, there are a million shades of gray, and it's okay to have flaws. Nobody is perfect.

- **Set manageable goals**

Set realistic goals. Break your overall goal into small, doable (preferably, one-day) projects. Otherwise, you could get overwhelmed and shut down. Start with something simple, like a character description. What is the protagonist like? What's the antagonist like?

Continue like this, setting goals that are attainable. Flesh out Act One. Give Act One a beginning, middle, and end. Break the act down into scenes, and so on. Don't write randomly; stick to a plan.

- **Don't sweat the small stuff**

I've known writers who get stuck on the small stuff. One particular writer I knew would type a sentence and then immediately start rewriting it. He wasn't following a plan. Writers like that will rewrite the same sentence six different ways.

Don't get hung up on details. Perfectionists tend to overwrite. Remember, it's the whole screenplay that matters, not every word. The perfect sentence isn't going to sell your script. Don't lose sight of the big picture. You'll make yourself crazy.

- **Nobody's born talented**

Some people think talent is something you're born with. They feel that you either have it or you don't. That's "all or nothing" thinking. You can't afford to think that way. You want to believe that your writing keeps getting better.

The more you practice writing, the better it will be. How do writers improve? They get feedback from better writers. They read screenplays. They go to movies.

- **Don't take everything personally**

Perfectionists tend to take every setback or criticism personally. Setbacks are supposed to be part of the process. For the perfectionist, though, setbacks can stop the process.

Don't let a bad writing day stifle your enthusiasm. Those days are going to happen. You want to be resilient. Set the screenplay aside and come back to it in a better frame of mind.

Don't give in to the perfectionist's worst nightmare: thinking your errors are evidence that you "aren't good enough." Bad days are expected. They don't prove you don't have talent. Don't give up. Take another look at your outline, stay the course, and bounce back.

- **The first draft is supposed to be rough**

The "shitty first draft" is the term Anne Lamott, author of *Bird By Bird*, came up with to trivialize the process of writing. Don't be overwhelmed by the rough draft. You want to think, "It's just a first attempt." It will get better.

Watch out for these kinds of perfectionist mind traps. Think about it. Writing just one screenplay takes time and focus. Over your career, you'll write dozens, maybe hundreds. With all that writing and rewriting, it'll be easy to get hung up on details.

It's easy to lose focus. Try not to overreact to setbacks. Keep everything in perspective.

I don't want you to get the wrong idea. I'm not advocating writers be sloppy or do shoddy work. You still need to be the healthy type of perfectionist. You still need to check all the boxes when you write a screenplay.

Don't overlook the important elements. The story has to make sense. The characters need to be flushed out. And yes, you absolutely have to catch all the spelling mistakes.

CHAPTER 21

Blocked? Remember Why You Started Writing

At some point in your screenwriting career, you will face a stretch when you just don't feel excited about writing. You might be just starting, and it's taking longer than you imagined to get that first break. You might be a working writer who hasn't sold a screenplay or landed a TV staff job in a while.

When that happens, your creative process can suffer. Going long stretches without selling anything can test your resolve. You might start to question your skills. What happens when you lose your motivation? What happens when you get blocked?

How do you recapture that initial excitement you felt about writing screenplays? If you're like most writers, you were inspired by watching great films or, in some cases, by a single movie. At the time, you undoubtedly had a favorite filmmaker, too. If you're anything like me, you rushed out to see every film they made.

And no doubt your favorite filmmakers had their favorite filmmakers. They also rushed out to see all of their favorite films. And more than likely, there was one fantastic film that stood out and inspired them just the way it did for you.

Quentin Tarantino found inspiration in the classic films he saw while working at that video rental store in Manhattan Beach. As the story goes, he was especially inspired by spaghetti westerns and Howard Hawk's *film noir* classics. It shows in films like *Django Unchained* and *Reservoir Dogs*.

An earlier generation of filmmakers was inspired by films like *Citizen Kane*. Filmmakers Martin Scorsese and Stanley Kubrick cite it as a film that inspired them. Both directors also include Fellini's *8½* in their list of film influences.

Known primarily for comedies, Woody Allen also lists those two films as inspirations. Allen has also clearly been influenced by two foreign directors, Frederico Fellini and Ingmar Bergman. Of course, he was inspired by comedies, too. He's explicitly mentioned that his favorite comedy was *Duck Soup* with the Marx Brothers.

Among independent filmmakers, Richard Linklater, writer of *A Boy's Life* and *Dazed and Confused,* says he was influenced by Robert Altman's *Nashville* and Francois Truffaut's *The 400 Blows*. Steven Soderberg, writer of *Sex, Lies, and Videotape,* lists among his influences Woody Allen's *Annie Hall* and Coppola's *The Godfather*.

When you're feeling stuck, try thinking about all the films that inspired you to start writing. What was it you loved about them? Did they have a strong social message? Did they feature especially moving performances? Did they create a suspenseful atmosphere? Think about how many times you watched them. What did that feel like?

When times get tough and you're not at your best, it's easy to forget. Don't forget how they made you feel. Find copies of your favorite film online, on a streaming network, or on DVD. Watch them again. Try to recall the excitement you felt when you first saw them.

List all the great movies and the gifted filmmakers who have inspired you over the years. Remember the skills you've brought to the table and all the other experiences that made you a better screenwriter. You might have forgotten somewhere along the way.

Then think about everything you've done since then to further your career. Did you make short films with your friends? Did you go to film school? Did you work on the set of a movie? At what point did you realize you could do it? Think about how those experiences felt. Get in touch with those emotions—they're the ones that inspired you to start.

Let them inspire you to keep writing.

CHAPTER 22

Fixes for Screenwriting Blocks

We sometimes forget how important it is to start with a great story idea for a screenplay. The concept has to grab the reader from the start and keep them turning pages. If the idea's not right, the script won't work.

There's a lot of pressure to "get it right" in the early stages of storytelling. What if you're stuck? What if your new idea suddenly sucks? You look for another idea, but nothing grabs you. You're blocked. You need a new idea.

Movie ideas can come from "true crime" forensic shows, other movies, graphic novels, and comic books. Check out newspapers, magazines, plays, and novels. Borrow from other sources. Find something you like, then change the characters, add some story twists, and make the story yours.

Experiment with ideas. Think of a compelling character, write a scene, and see if it suggests a story. Write about a friend dealing with a problem, a drug addiction, or a breakup. Write about how your first marriage went sideways.

Write stories about characters from your favorite films. What happens to the Sandra Bullock character before or after the end of *Gravity*? What happens to the Casey Affleck character a year after *Manchester by the Sea*? What happens if Juliet survives and Romeo doesn't?

What if you've come up with a great idea but can't see the movie yet? You feel like it should be better. What happened? Think about how to push the concept. Make it stronger. Raise the stakes. Throw more obstacles at the hero. Come up with a stronger antagonist.

Watch some movies in your genre. Read the summaries of similar films on the Internet Movie Database (IMDB). Borrow from the greats. Every writer does it. There are no new stories, after all, just different ways to spin them.

Rethink Your Story Dynamics

What if you find yourself forcing things to work story-wise? If the story dynamics were great to begin with, the second and third acts would tend to flow freely. Some movies get written in a week, like *Rocky* or *Taxi Driver*. What if your story doesn't flow?

Make sure your characters have strong motives. Rocky was just another bum from the neighborhood who made it to the World Heavyweight Championships. He loved his turtles, Cuff and Link. He was a huge long shot, but he never gave up.

Bonnie and Clyde were cool, good-looking bank robbers. People loved them because they were folk heroes. They stole from the rich. *The Silence of the Lambs* had the creepiest villain ever. A brilliant psychiatrist who also happened to be a cannibal. If you're stuck on a story, listen to your characters. What do they want?

If you're writing a comedy, check your characters. Do they have funny attitudes? Eddie Murphy in *Beverly Hills*

Cop was disrespectful, flippant, and constantly bent the rules. Check your story. Is your story inherently funny? Is your hero possessed by the persona of John Malkovich? Does he dress in drag on a police assignment like in *Big Mama's House?*

Is your hero inherently vulnerable? Look at the heroes in *Wait Until Dark* and *Rear Window*. Blind and crippled. Think about your protagonist and your antagonist. Pick the most exciting combination. Erin Brockovich was a poor, struggling, gum-chewing bottle-blonde who took down the gazillionaire CEOs at Pacific Gas and Electric.

Examine what your protagonist wants, both externally and internally. Let those drives show you where your story lies. Take a good look at your antagonist, too. Look at the themes that run through their character arcs. Let your story prove the premise. Does love conquer all? Does power corrupt? Show how that happens.

When the Fear of Judgment Kicks In

You're not happy with what you've written. You're hypercritical of your work. You think about trashing your script. Okay, first, all writers are hypercritical. We're all afraid of being judged.

Realize you're just like the rest of us. You've got to write through the self-doubt. If every writer who doubted themselves gave up, there wouldn't be any writers. You could start another project. You might need a break. Some perspective. After a while, go back to your script. You'll have fresh eyes.

Another way: If that inner critic is too loud, drown it out. That critic will be necessary for the rewrite, but while you're breaking the story, blast the Stones. Led Zepplin. Mozart. Whatever works.

Don't let self-doubt stop you. What is negative self-talk? You'll recognize it as questions such as:

"Why does my script suck?"

"Why did I ever think I could do this?"

"I guess I'm just not good enough."

When negative self-talk occurs, stop, get up, and do something else. Make coffee. Surf the net. Whatever you do, don't obsess about it. Self-critical thought is the enemy of all creativity. Catch it. Stop. Center yourself, clear your head, and write.

Getting Back Into Flow

The average screenwriter writes about three to six pages a day. You might get lucky and get into a "flow" state that allows you to write 15 straight pages of really high-quality material.

You have a great day. You go to sleep feeling good about your script. Somehow, the next morning, you're stuck. The following dozen pages feel boring, awkward, or stilted. You've lost the flow.

Go back to your outline. Read it through from the top. Try to figure out where it stalled out. You might get lucky and recapture the "flow"—this happens to me all the time. I'll go back to the outline, read it through, and when I get to the weak part, a new idea occurs to me. It's the momentum effect.

If that doesn't work, you might need a break. Clear your head. Tomorrow, it might all come together. Give it a few days and think of new twists or fresh dialogue. Think about raising the stakes—or jacking up the conflict.

If that doesn't help, you might have to abandon some of the material, even the excellent stuff, and go a different way. You could introduce a new character. It could be that your hero isn't the hero at all. He might be a minor character. Sometimes, a new direction can get you back on track.

If you're still stuck, try putting everything away and rewriting from scratch. Same story, same scenes, new words. Don't look at the old stuff. Read it over, get the gist, and then start again. Get back into the flow.

Another approach, if you're stuck, is to look ahead and find a scene that seems more fun to write. Write that one. Pick another. Any scene that appeals to you. Write that one next. Keep it up until you're done. Then, put all the scenes together like a puzzle.

Something I do when I feel lost in the script—I'll write a summary of the story. It's easy to lose sight of the story in a full screenplay. Sometimes, it helps to shrink the story. Write it all out in a page. Read it over. Get a feeling for the entirety of the storyline.

What If Nothing Works?

After a break, you still don't see the fix. Okay, maybe this just isn't the best idea. Don't give up yet. You're probably too close. This is when you ask a friend to read it.

Don't ask your mom to read it. She's going to say she loves it. Same with your girlfriend. Ask your screenwriting friends. If you get good feedback, great. Consider their ideas. If a number of your friends have the same comments, take them seriously.

If there's no consensus among your writer friends, check with a professional screenwriting consultant. If they have ideas for fixes that resonate with you, keep writing. If you've tried everything and are still stuck—it's time to move on. There's no shame in that. It's happened to every writer ever.

Of course, as soon as you give up on your story, just wait—six months later, an idea "so close" to yours will get greenlit and become a box office smash.

CHAPTER 23

Coping with Rejection

Think about what you go through every day as a writer. You have to pour your heart and soul into your scripts. And they can't *just* be good, either. They have to be amazing to get the studios' attention. So, you spend all your waking free time on it. You do your absolute best.

After all that, your script gets rejected. It feels awful. How do you cope? You feel angry and then depressed. Or the other way around. It's okay to feel the pain; it's part of the healing process. Go ahead, feel it. Just to be safe—put away the sharp objects.

It's not just about the writing. If you're not independently wealthy, you have to work a day job driving for Uber Eats or whatever. If you're in a relationship, you must find time to be a good partner. You have to pay the rent, gas, power, and electric. You have to put food on the table.

Think about the odds you're up against. The studios only make a few hundred movies every year, while they get thousands of script submissions.

We talked about the mantra: "Every writer goes through it." It's true. I've never heard of a writer who didn't get a ton of rejections. You're not alone. It helps to remember that you're in good company.

It's a Numbers Game

Ok, so you've processed the pain. You're getting over the fact that your script didn't sell. Now, it's time to let go. Stop feeling sorry for yourself.

Are you having trouble getting motivated to write again? Give yourself reasons to keep writing. One thing I try to focus on is that it's a numbers game. Each new screenplay you write gives you another turn at bat. The more you write, the better your chances.

Another good mantra, "You can get a thousand no*s*; you only need one yes."

Keep Rejection in Perspective with Everything Else in Life

You've experienced rejection before. You've been around for a long time and didn't always get your way. You didn't make the football team. You asked that cheerleader out and got shut down. Some other girl has stolen your date. You didn't get accepted at USC.

All these things happened. You survived. Writing just happens to be what you're most passionate about right now. A lot is riding on each submission. So, the rejections sting a lot more.

You survived a lot of disappointment in your life. You got past it all somehow. Think about how you dealt with those rejections. Did you throw yourself into your next project? Did you leave town for a week?

Coping with Rejection

You've got to shake it off.

Picture Yourself Overcoming Rejection

When I told one of my college professors that I wanted to be a screenwriter, he laughed, then said I was crazy, and then he laughed some more. Eventually, he suggested that I "visualize it."

He actually said, "Visualize it, and it will probably happen." It sounded weird at the time, but it turned out to be great advice. I tried it. And a few years later, I ended up writing for TV.

Visualize your success. Visualize yourself writing a bunch of awesome screenplays. Picture yourself working with a famous producer. Picture yourself accepting an Oscar from Scarlett Johansson. Don't visualize the rejections.

Constructive Criticism Can Help You Grow as a Writer

Sometimes, the criticism you get from the studios can be enlightening. If it's worthwhile criticism, you'll want to pay attention to it. Lots of writers have rewritten their scripts after a rejection with positive results.

You should take a look at the studio notes. Normally, you'd have to pay good money to get that kind of feedback from an executive or a story analyst. As always, use your judgment. If you don't agree with their notes, toss them.

Don't Let the Rejections Kill Your Career

Writers can become so jaded by the process and, frankly, so afraid of the odds that they decide to stop writing altogether.

With the chances of selling a screenplay so low, why bother? Maybe it's time to think about teaching.

How do you keep your spirits up? You've got to celebrate your victories. What victories, you say? Well, try writing for web series, shorts, graphic novels, and plays. Try to write something that will get produced. Get some confidence as a working writer, then branch out.

If your script places highly in a contest, gets you an agent, gets you hired to write a project, or gets optioned or bought, those are all successes. Savor the victories, even the small ones. Focus on them, not the failures—and keep writing.

CHAPTER 24

How Writers Process the Pain

When one of your screenplays gets rejected, it's only natural that you'll go through a mourning process. You've invested so much psychic energy over so much time, coming up with the idea, outlining it, breaking it down into scenes, fleshing out character arcs, and writing draft after draft—and it all comes down to … what?

"Sorry, it's not for us."

Every morning, you've been getting up at 5 a.m. to write before you go to work. You've been guzzling coffee and eating off the two-dollar menu at McDonalds. You've hardly spent any time with your wife or kids for … what?

"We already have something like this in the pipeline."

After all your sacrifice and emotional commitment, you finally get to the point where you feel your script is really good. Your hopes are high. They have to be. A lot is riding on each script you send out.

You turn it over to someone who's expressed an interest—an agent, maybe a producer. Then, while you're waiting the longest three weeks ever to hear back—you let yourself imagine that they loved it. You allow yourself to fantasize about a scenario where they offer to buy it. Or at least option it.

Then the phone rings, and you hear the bad news …

"The dialogue was stiff, clumsy, and felt 'written.' The characters felt flat. The story petered out in the second act."

When you hear those words, it's no surprise you'll feel a significant loss. Without sounding overly dramatic, it may take you a while to get over it. It's going to hurt. How do you get over it? To process a loss, they say you need to "sit with the emotions."

That means don't just sweep your feelings under the rug. When you keep emotions bottled up, they tend to fester. If they're not expressed or felt, resentments will build and build—and, one day, you'll blow up a studio.

When you first hear that your script has been passed over, it might not even register. You might think, "There must be some mistake." If you're reading a rejection letter, you might have to reread it. If it's an assistant on the phone, you might stop them and ask, "Are you sure?"

Eventually, you will accept the truth—and it will hurt. You'll want to lash out at whoever read your script. Probably some guy with no talent at all. The best job he could get was reading other people's scripts and bashing them mercilessly.

Don't project your feelings onto innocent bystanders. Don't kick the dog or lash out at your neighbor or kids, no matter how conveniently they're available. You do need to vent. Vent to another writer. Spare your wife. Hasn't she put up with enough of your crap already? All she does is support you—don't make her rethink it.

You might stay up all night thinking about it and decide—wait, maybe they made a mistake. Writers have been known to call the producer to convince them they were wrong. "Didn't you get the message I was trying to convey? Maybe if you just read it again."

I don't recommend you do this. Producers will rarely reread a script. Once they've passed, they're not changing their minds. Don't piss them off—you might want to send them another script someday.

Some writers will try to offer the producer a free rewrite. This might actually be a good idea, especially if the rejection came with some specific area that needed work. Most likely, it won't change anything, but you never know. Reread the rejection. See if you can determine if they were "on the fence" or just hated it.

Whatever you do, don't just do the rewrite and send it back. This is not a good idea. Don't resubmit the same script without talking to the producer first. Give them a choice. You don't want to burn the bridge with this person.

Sometimes, the rejection strikes at your core. Self-doubt starts creeping in. You might find yourself questioning your career choice. "What was I thinking? I should have gone to law school." Next comes day drinking and binging detective shows on Netflix.

Writers have been known to give up on writing altogether. After 13 rejections, you can easily lose hope. Don't let yourself wallow in self-pity. You might do something really stupid, like actually go to law school or go after that job working at your uncle's car dealership. Whatever you do, don't allow that to happen!

Give it some time. You'll get over it. "Every writer goes through it"—that's your mantra. Pretty soon, you'll find hope in moving forward. You might see a film that blows you away. You might feel inspired to write again. Of course, it might work the other way. You might see a film that sucks so badly you'll just have to write another script.

SECTION 3

BREAKING IN—DAY JOBS

CHAPTER 25

Best Day Jobs for Writers

A problem facing all aspiring screenwriters is paying the rent while struggling to write. The usual entry-level day jobs here in Los Angeles, such as a barista, cab driver, restaurant server or bartender, or on-call dogwalker, can be physically and emotionally exhausting.

When you finally have time to knock off a few pages, you're hardly at your best.

What about getting a day job working on a studio lot or at a production company? You'd be working in the entertainment industry. You'd be working closely with people like yourself. Depending on which studio, you might get free admission to the theme park.

Story Analyst

One of my favorite jobs was evaluating and writing script coverage at American International Pictures. I learned how to cover scripts in a class at USC, then went out and got a job the same semester. The work involved reading a screenplay or a novel each day and writing a tight synopsis for the executives higher up to read.

We also had to rate the script's concept, setting, and production values, as well as review the storyline, plot structure, character, dialogue, and pacing from "poor" to "excellent." You learn a lot about how to write a screenplay. You also learn a valuable lesson—90% of screenplays are really, really bad.

To get this job, you'll need a working knowledge of the three-act structure and other basics of screenwriting. Where do you pick up this knowledge? I learned from a class on story analysis in film school. You can also learn by taking extension courses or reading books like *Screenplay—The Foundations of Screenwriting* by Syd Field. It definitely helps if you've written a few feature-length spec scripts, too.

As a story analyst, you will also work closely with people who have the power to greenlight a project.

Production Assistant

While trying to break into writing, I also worked as a production assistant (PA), driving film canisters for TV and film projects around to film labs, screening rooms, and studio executives' garish mansions in Malibu.

While it's definitely an entry-level job, you'd be amazed at how many successful producers, directors, writers, and even actors started this way.

For example, Kathleen Kennedy, President of Lucasfilm and recipient of multiple Academy Award nominations, began as a PA for John Milius. Her connections from various PA jobs eventually led her to produce films with Steven Spielberg and George Lucas. Today, she produces films with her husband, Frank Marshall.

Writer's Assistant

This is, by far, the best day job you can get. By far! Especially if you want to write for television. If you're good at it, this job can get you your first writing credit. It can kickstart your entire career.

There are writer's assistant positions outside of TV, too. Lots of feature writers are looking for writing assistants. Those jobs can be great as well. All these positions put you in close contact with working writers.

The thing about being a writer's assistant in TV is that you work in the writer's room with the writing staff. Your job is to take notes while the other writers pitch story ideas and jokes until 2 a.m. every night. Sounds great, doesn't it?

Back in the day, I was lucky enough to co-create a couple of half-hour TV shows. As co-creator and executive producer, my partner and I were able to hire a talented writer's assistant. Working with us every day, he quickly learned the show.

Every once in a while, he'd pitch a joke. Some of them were funny. We eventually rewarded him with a script assignment. When you sell a script on a TV show, agents will be happy to represent you. So, he got his first writing credit and an agent.

Eventually, he landed a job on *SpongeBob SquarePants*, based on the script he wrote for our show. His writing career started to take off. Later, he became a showrunner on another animated show, for which he won an Emmy.

We gave another assistant the same opportunity. He got his first writing credit on our show. After the show wrapped, he landed a job on *Dexter*. He worked there for seven years and was promoted to executive producer.

How do you get a writer's assistant job? You must submit a spec for a television show or an original pilot. For obvious reasons, every aspiring TV writer in town wants this gig. It helps (a lot) if you know somebody, so networking is essential.

You're going to have to pay the rent, somehow. You might as well look into some of these entry-level studio jobs. If you play your cards right, you might work closely with people who can literally make your career.

However, since I started writing this book, this has changed a bit. Unfortunately, the way TV works today, with streamers like Netflix and Prime, there are smaller staffs. And I've heard opportunities are not as great as they have been for writing assistants. I still think it's one of the best ways to get your first paid writing job.

CHAPTER 26
Famous Screenwriter's Day Jobs

Before they were famous, these writers all started out like you. They had an idea for a screenplay. They came to Hollywood, London, or other places known for making movies. They wrestled with the same issues—motivation, focus, and discipline. And, just like you, they needed jobs.

J.K. Rowling
Rowling is known for writing what is probably the most popular series of young adult novels of all time: the *Harry Potter* books. She has written screenplays adapted from some of her other books, including her five-part *Fantastic Beasts and Where to Find Them* series. She's written screenplay adaptations for some of her other works, including *The Casual Vacancy*.

Rowling has talked about being "on the dole" in the UK and being a depressed and even suicidal single mother while writing some of her early works.

As a teenager, she tried to get into Oxford but was rejected. She eventually was accepted by Exeter, from which she graduated in 1986.

After that, she worked as a researcher and translator for Amnesty International. She worked at the Manchester Chamber of Commerce when she started writing *Harry Potter*.

David O. Russell

Russell wrote and directed independent films such as *Flirting with Disaster* and *Spanking the Monkey*. At some point, he graduated to more mainstream films, like *Three Kings*, later writing and directing Academy Award-nominated films like *Silver Linings Playbook, Joy*, and *American Hustle*.

Russell wrote and directed a very impressive list of films featuring quirky, funny characters and original, unpredictable storylines.

Russell's early day jobs included a slew of equally unimpressive service jobs such as waiting tables and tending bar. However, his major in English and Political Science at Amherst groomed him for more serious pursuits, like teaching in a literacy program in Nicaragua, political activism, and community organization. Eventually, he landed his first media job as an intern with *Smithsonian World* for PBS.

James Cameron

Everybody knows Cameron for the *Terminator* film series and his box office-shattering and critically acclaimed Oscar-winning films *Titanic* and *Avatar*. Before all that, however, he grew up in Orange County and studied physics at Cal State Fullerton.

At some point, his interests changed, and he switched his major to English and then dropped out. Back when he was still dreaming of a film career, he worked at a machine shop and became a school bus driver and a truck driver.

Cameron was a genius at designing aliens and monsters and found a job working as a miniature model maker at the Roger Corman Studios. There, he got the chance to direct his first commercial film, *Piranha II*. Unfortunately, he was unceremoniously fired off the film by some hack producer.

Stephen King

King is widely known for his novels, including *Carrie, The Shining, The Stand, Misery,* and *Rita Hayworth and The Shawshank Redemption.* All of those novels have been adapted for film. King wrote the screenplays for the movies *Pet Sematary, Creepshow,* and the television miniseries *The Shining.*

When he first started out, however, he worked various odd jobs, including gas pump attendant, laundry worker, and high school janitor, which is where he was inspired to write the novel *Carrie.*

Still a struggling writer, King earned a teaching certificate that allowed him to teach high school. Since he couldn't find a teaching job immediately, he started selling short stories to magazines such as *Cavalier.*

He eventually landed a teaching job at Hampden Academy in Maine. While teaching, he finished the manuscript for *Carrie,* for which he received an advance of $2,500.

John Patrick Shanley

Shanley is the Academy Award-winning screenwriter of *Moonstruck* and the Pulitzer Prize-winning playwright for *Doubt.* He also wrote the screenplay for the film version of *Doubt.*

Shanley enlisted in the Marines during the Vietnam War. However, he never saw active duty, being stationed in the

States. After the Marines, Shanley attended college and then worked as an elevator operator, house painter, bartender, and moving man.

Richard Linklater

Linklater wrote and directed some classic independent films, including *Dazed and Confused, Slackers, Before Midnight, and Waking Life*. Eventually, he wrote and directed the Oscar-nominated film *Boyhood*.

Growing up in Huntsville, Texas, his first day job was parking cars at the local prison rodeo. At that point, he dreamed of becoming the first professional baseball player/serious novelist.

After the baseball/novelist dream went by the wayside, he found work on an oil rig off the shore of Houston for about two years.

Aaron Sorkin

Sorkin has written a lot of dramatic films, including *A Few Good Men, The American President, Steve Jobs,* and the Academy Award-winning Best Picture *The Social Network*.

After graduating from Syracuse University with a degree in Musical Theater, he became just another struggling writer, working day jobs such as a limousine driver, tending bar, handing out fliers for a hunting and fishing show, and delivering singing telegrams.

After the Broadway and film success of *A Few Good Men*, Sorkin landed the ultimate "day job" as a contract writer for Castle Rock, doing rewrites and polishes, working under the mentorship of Academy Award-winning screenwriter William Goldman.

Famous Screenwriter's Day Jobs

Even the best, most successful, and most famous writers you've admired and whose movies you've loved had to work mundane jobs to get by while writing in their free time.

They've all made sacrifices and struggled to pay the rent. Some had families to support, working all day and finding an hour here or there to write. They scrounged up time to write in the early mornings or into the night. They didn't wait for inspiration. They couldn't afford to.

I was curious to see how the best screenwriters broke into the business. The answer is that they found time to write, made contacts, and found the jobs they needed to get by.

The point? Everybody does it—and not just these writers. Every writer, ever (unless they were trust fund babies), struggled with the rent. Again—it's not just you.

SECTION 4

BREAKING IN—FOR OLDER WRITERS

CHAPTER 27

How Old Is Too Old for Hollywood?

There are some writers who've broken into Hollywood later in life. Julian Fellowes wrote *Gosford Park* at 52. David Seidler wrote *Malice in Wonderland* at age 46. Courtney Hunt wrote *Frozen River* at age 44. Guillermo Arriaga wrote *Amores Perros* at age 42. David Peoples wrote *Blade Runner* at age 42.

The unfortunate truth is there is ageism in Hollywood. However, that doesn't mean writers in their 50s can't get jobs or writing assignments. It just means your chances get harder, especially if you're over 40. But it can be done.

First, let's examine why ageism happens.

To clarify, this chapter should really be titled *How Old Is Too Old to Start Writing for Hollywood?* If you start in your 20s or 30s, you can write as long as you can hold on to your career.

How can you hold onto your career?

If you can keep writing for 20 years straight, you will likely continue working in Hollywood as long as you're still writing professionally. Actually, scratch that. As long as your writing is as good or better than everyone else's. This is partly a matter of luck.

For example, if you write for TV and keep getting jobs on shows that only last a year, your chances of having a short career increase.

If you get lucky, and your first job is on a huge hit show like *The Simpsons*, you'll likely move up from staff writer to story editor, to producer, and eventually, to executive producer. You could be on that show for many, many years. Of course, you have to consistently write at the level of the show or better.

However, if your scripts are subpar and continually being rewritten, if you don't seem to be capturing the characters' voices or the tone of the show, you will most likely not be asked back at the end of the season. But if you're good enough, you'll keep moving up.

If you work on a string of shows that are canceled in their first year, you don't get known for being a writer on a hit show. This puts you in a lesser category. Producers and network executives consider you a "B" show writer.

So, you don't become the first choice on the next show. It's a self-fulfilling prophecy. You keep getting hired on "B" shows.

There is a way out of this. Sell a script to an "A" show. For example, recent "A" shows include *The Crown*, *The Handmaid's Tale*, *Curb Your Enthusiasm*, and *Better Call Saul*. Any show with an Emmy nomination for writing is a safe bet.

Even selling one episode on those shows will help you reach "A" show levels.

There's another factor. In Hollywood, everyone's asking, "What have you done lately? If you go two years without selling a script, studios and networks start to forget about you. That's how careers begin to end.

And in feature screenwriting, it's much harder to sell consistently. As I've mentioned elsewhere in this book, so few feature film scripts are bought by studios these days. It's hard to keep selling year after year.

Why is that? At least half the movies made today are superhero films, kid's films, prequels, sequels, remakes, or based on various forms of intellectual property. Those films are considered lower risk because they have a built-in audience.

The studios are going to give those scripts to their tried-and-true best writers.

There's another reason it's harder to get hired in TV if you're older. The average age of showrunners and network executives is generally between 35 to 45 years old. There are some older showrunners, of course, which helps. A 35-year-old showrunner will feel awkward about giving notes to a writer in his 50s or 60s.

Most of the writers on a TV staff will be 25 to 35. Maybe 40. So, executive producers want a writers' room where people get along and socialize with each other. So, the 35-year-old showrunner will try to keep the age range down.

Studios and networks also favor younger writers. They have lists of "up-and-coming" writers. They love to discover young, new talent.

There is also a perception that younger writers relate better to younger audiences and come up with "fresher" ideas. This may not be true, but that's what people think. In TV, advertisers want to reach young adults. It's a crucial age. They want their ads to reach young couples who haven't developed "brand preferences" yet.

Advertisers want to influence young adults to start buying Volvos. Why? That's when consumers develop brand loyalty. There's a chance they'll remain Volvo customers for life, and their kids will pick up on it ultimately.

In TV and features, there's a preconceived notion that may or may not be true: Many of the people who go to movies are dating, so again, young adults. Lots of movies come out each year, especially romantic comedies meant to draw in teens and young adults.

Think about date movies. They're often "young adult" films like *The Hunger Games*, *Maze Runner*, or any romantic comedy with Jennifer Lawrence.

There's also a huge children's market for films. When kids find out about these movies, like *Cinderella* or other Disney or Pixar films, they don't stop screaming until their parents take them to see the latest kid pic. Parents can't fight it.

This explains the thinking behind Hollywood's tendency to hire "new young writers." It's like a bad habit that's hard to give up. It's the way things have been done.

It's all BS. The truth is, a 60-year-old writer can write a great young adult feature or a romantic comedy. They can write anything a 20-year-old can write. Unfortunately, studio execs are trained not to think that way.

Don't give up. You can make it in this town if you're starting out over 50. It's just a bit harder. Finally, it's the words on the page that matter.

You might look at it this way: your odds of making it in screenwriting are astronomical. How much worse can it be for an older writer? Don't give up, especially if you love writing.

CHAPTER 28

How to Break in as an Older Writer

What are some ways older writers can find help trying to break in? Write a great spec script for an existing show and a great TV pilot. There are workshops designed to help older writers.

For example, there is the Warner Brothers Writers Workshop and the CBS Diversity Institute (which has a Diversity Mentoring Program for older writers). There's also a Disney/ABC Writing Program, a program called the Fox Diversity Program, and the NBC Diversity Initiative for Writers.

Diversity is defined by the Writers Guild of America as minority writers, writers with disabilities, women, gay and lesbian writers, and writers over 55. The industry is aware of the ageism in Hollywood and has taken some small steps to correct it.

Older writers should also take advantage of writing contests. When you submit your script, you don't have to list your age. The playing field is more even. Some contests tend to carry more weight than others.

You'll also have a better chance of breaking in if you've been writing plays or novels. Even if you're not famous, a track record of writing will help you. If you're famous, your chances of selling scripts go up.

For example, the famous novelist Raymond Chandler sold his first screenplay at age 56. His first big novel, *The Big Sleep*, was published at 51. He co-wrote the screenplay for *Double Indemnity* with Billy Wilder at age 56.

Julian Fellowes sold *Gosford Park* at age 52. While he was not a writer before writing the script, Fellowes was an actor who had many high-level contacts. He has since created the classic show *Downton Abbey* and several other TV shows and movies.

Older Writers in Television

Usually, networks like to buy TV pilots from showrunners or writers who've been on TV writing staffs for years. They want a showrunner with a proven track record. This doesn't bode well for the writer looking for their first TV job over 50.

There is a possible scenario in which you, as an older writer with no TV writing credits, can get your pilot on the air. If the executives at the studios and networks are so blown away by the quality of your pilot script, they may pair you up with a proven showrunner.

Another factor that can work to your advantage is the older showrunner. For example, when David Chase was running *The Sopranos*, he was in his 60s. If he absolutely loved a great TV spec script written by a 57-year-old writer, it wouldn't be that awkward for him to hire you. There's very little age difference.

Older Writers in Feature Films

In many ways, if you're over 50, you have a better chance of breaking in by writing feature film scripts than writing for television. TV is more geared toward younger writers. However, there are exceptions to every rule.

Some advice for any novice writer: look at the world of low-budget filmmaking. In that world, the words on the page matter more than anybody's age. These producers and directors are just looking for the best script they can find to produce a low-budget feature that can break through and jump-start their careers. Remember, these are non-union jobs and pay considerably less than WGA signatories.

However, you may find that you can succeed at that level, where there is less ageism, and leverage that success to get better-paying jobs. Success at any level bodes well for success at every level.

If you're fortunate, you'll be one of those older people who still looks, acts, talks, and dresses younger. If you can "pass" for younger, you have a significant advantage. If you're grey, bald, have wrinkles, walk with a limp, or have some other affliction, then it's going to be more challenging. You have to be a really, really great writer. You can't just be "good enough."

I remember going into a staffing meeting after a basketball injury. I needed a cane to get around. My agent at the time freaked out. She couldn't believe I took the meeting and brought the cane with me, but I got the job anyway.

Another possibility is that if you can't find work in TV or film, you may want to funnel your creativity into publishing a novel or mounting a play. People in the theater appear to be much less ageist. Books can be self-published. You might find a local theater interested in your play.

Another thing: writing plays or novels makes it more likely to see your work produced. And that's really one of the best reasons to write.

You never know; a film producer might just read your novel or see your play and decide to make it into a movie.

SECTION 5

CAREER STRATEGIES—GET OUT OF YOUR COMFORT ZONE

CHAPTER 29

Hang Out with More Successful Writers

If you're trying to break into writing for television or film, chances are you're already hanging around with other writers. If you don't have friends who are going after the goals you are, get some new friends.

It's not that complicated. Join some groups, get out, and meet other writers. You can do it. You have to decide you want to do it first. Then, you take the logical next steps.

If you can manage it, try to make friends with writers who are just a bit more successful than you. It's clearly more intimidating to hang out with really successful writers. You know who I'm talking about. You don't have to meet those guys right away.

There's probably someone in your screenwriting class who's placed very high up in—let's say—the Page screenwriting competition. That's a guy you want to get to know better. Offer to buy them coffee and find out how they did it.

What happens when you start hanging around with others who've had some success? If you're smart, you listen to them. Ask questions. Find out where they got the idea for their script. Which screenwriting books do they like? Do they have an agent or a manager? How did they make that happen?

Where do you find writers who've achieved some success but not too much? You can find them working on laptops in coffee shops and bars. You can find them at seminars, contests, and pitchfests. Even if you can't find an actual person to hang around with, you can find other writers online.

Writers who've experienced some success are generally happy to share their secrets.

Like all writers, they've struggled and overcome some steep odds. Let them share their stories with you. How did they write every day? What was their ritual?

As you get to know writers who've experienced some success, you'll pick up on how confident they are about writing. Those feelings can be contagious. When you see someone you know achieve their goals, you feel you can do it, too.

Put yourself out there. Meet some other screenwriters. There are thousands of them in LA. Make some friends. Meet for coffee every once in a while. Share movie ideas with them. At some point, you'll exchange scripts and give each other feedback.

The guys who are the furthest ahead of you in their careers will have the most valuable feedback. When you read their scripts, you'll better understand how to do it right. You can discuss what works and what doesn't. After a while, you're both bound to get better.

Hopefully, you and your friends will reach professional levels in screenwriting at about the same time. And if you keep in touch, you can help each other throughout your careers.

Hang Out with More Successful Writers

Early in our careers, my partner and I connected with some of the most talented writers in writing classes. There were two guys in particular, Bob and Howard Bendetson. We were all interested in writing TV comedies, and we broke in together about the same time.

We kept in touch and ended up working on some of the same shows, including *The Jeffersons, Alice, Newhart,* and *Alf.* In fact, they helped us get some of those jobs. That's the way it's supposed to work.

When you get close to a more successful writer, you start to see that succeeding is possible. After all, it's just someone in your class. All this time, you thought they were a loser. But somehow, they placed high in the Page competition and got an agent. Hanging around with this person will help you feel you can do it too. Success *is* possible.

CHAPTER 30

Networking Advice for Screenwriters

When you go to an event to meet other writers, have your priorities straight. Don't go to the event expecting to sell your script. That's not going to happen. Don't go in expecting favors from other writers. First, you create a relationship. You nurture it. You stay in touch.

Think about what you can offer the writers you meet. Maybe you have a screenwriting book they'd like to borrow. Maybe you have a screenplay they'd like to read. You could recommend a great writing class or a great writing coach. Share your career strategies.

Where are they coming from? What do you have in common? What are their goals? What kind of scripts do they write? Don't talk about you the whole time—be interested in what they have to say. Remember, you're there to forge a friendship. You're playing the "long game."

You're attending this event to nurture relationships with other writers and industry professionals who will be helpful and even necessary in your future career.

I can't emphasize this enough. At first, networking is about how you can help the other person. It's not about you. It's what you can do for others. That's the right mindset.

Follow Up on the First Meeting

When you get home, jot down some interesting things about the people you met. Just some personal details or something interesting they said to remember them by.

If you want to be more organized, when you get home, you can type up a networking list or add names to your phone contact list.

You might want to make a note to try to reach your new contacts by phone sometime in the next month. Not too soon. Or, your next move could be to email the person you met, saying how much you enjoyed meeting and getting to know them.

Set Up a Coffee Meeting with Your Contact and Keep in Touch

If everything seems to be on track, you may suggest a meeting for coffee or a drink. You might want to practice a 20-second pitch for two or three screenplay ideas.

At coffee, remember to be entertaining and calm; don't push. However, if the opportunity presents itself, you could mention a couple of ideas. If the reaction is right, you can go further and offer to send an outline or script.

Later, you might want to touch base with these people by sending an individual email every couple of months. Another idea—you could write a weekly or monthly blog about your current projects and entertaining adventures in Hollywood and keep your contacts on the e-mail list.

Networking is an anxiety-provoking but necessary activity for anyone aspiring to Hollywood jobs.

It's especially difficult for writers, who aren't known for being outgoing and comfortable around large groups. Knowing what to expect from the experience will, in itself, reduce the stress involved. Give it some thought before you go. Be prepared.

Set a modest networking goal for each event—nothing too extreme. For example, you could exchange phone numbers with three people or introduce yourself to six people and find out what they do in the film business.

You might go to a meeting of micro-budget filmmakers and offer to help on set or as a production assistant.

Don't worry if you've only accomplished modest goals. You'll find it gets easier the more you do it.

You'll have opportunities to strengthen your relationships the more you see some of the same people, and they may be able to introduce you to their friends in the business.

Be on Your Best Behavior

You need to keep your wits about you. You want to move the conversation in the right direction.

No matter who you're talking to, don't be negative or controversial. You don't know where the person you're talking to stands on any subject. Don't assume.

Remember to talk with the guests, not just the "players."

If you have trouble with small talk, focus on what's happening at the event. Talk about the food or the cool-looking ice sculpture. Don't be negative. What if the ice sculptor is the host's best friend? Don't mock his work.

Feel free to discuss current hit movies, TV shows, or writers you admire. Don't interview the person; make casual small talk. See how it goes, and if they start talking more, you can proceed to more personal topics.

Whatever you do, don't spend the whole conversation talking about yourself. Ask questions about the people you speak with. Let them talk about themselves while you remain interested. Stay positive.

You need to know when to move on. If the person you're talking with seems bored, checks their watch, or stares off into space, it could be a sign to move on. Cut your losses.

Talking to a Celebrity

If you're talking to someone you've heard of, prepare to talk about their films. Always be positive. Ask questions. Ask a specific question like, "I really liked that film. How did you get close enough to film that rhino?"

Try to act like a working professional. Give the impression you've been writing freelance screenplays for a while. Don't ask them to take a "selfie" with you or autograph a book. Act like you're used to seeing celebrities like them. Don't come off like a tourist.

Don't Hand Your Script to Anyone at the Event

Even if the person you're talking to asks if they can read your screenplay, don't give it to them at the event (even if you have a trunkload of scripts in your car). This sends a message that you're desperate.

The best case scenario is to tell people you'll call your manager in the morning and have them send over the script.

If you don't have representation, get their contact information and email it the next day.

Be Well-Informed About Movies and TV

Depending on the networking event you're going to, you need preparation. What if you know who you're going to meet? Check their IMDB page. Watch a movie they've written or produced.

Keep up with popular films and TV shows. You've got to know your market. You'll need a general working knowledge of who does what in Hollywood. Make it your business to learn about current actors, directors, writers, agents, and producers.

You can get some of this information by reading the *Hollywood Reporter, Daily Variety,* and the *Calendar* section of the *LA Times*. You can also watch TV shows like *Extra, Entertainment Tonight,* or even *TMZ*.

Being well-informed will give you confidence and reduce stress because you'll have some go-to subjects for conversation.

CHAPTER 31

Best Places to Network

There are lots of places screenwriters like to hang out—including bars, coffee shops, restaurants, tattoo parlors, on the bus, at the beach, and just about anywhere else you can carry a laptop.

There are workshops, seminars, webinars, writers' groups, and writing classes. Some events are held solely to meet other writers. These include lectures, Q&As, panel discussions, breakfasts, coffees, cocktail hours, brunches, parties, and retreats.

You can also find other screenwriters online. For example, you can find them on LinkedIn. Hundreds of screenwriters and TV writers are listed on the site. Among the groups represented are The Scriptwriter's Network, Stage 32, and The Writers' Club of Los Angeles.

You can go to MeetUp.com. You'll find the South Bay Screenwriters 2.0 and Santa Monica Writers and Screenwriters. You'll also find groups like Write Out Loud!, which embraces LGBTQ writers. Other examples are Write It Up!, Ink Tank, and Writers Blok.

On Facebook, you can find lots of screenwriting groups. For example, The Craft of Screenwriting, The Art of Story,

Thirty Day Screenplay, LA TV Writers, 1 Page a Day, Writing in the Modern World, Screenwriting, and one of my favorites, Hippie-Dippie Hollywood Hopefuls, run by my good friend Mark Gunnion.

What goes on in these Facebook groups?
Members argue about the best screenwriting software (the answer is "FinalDraft"). They argue whether the screenwriting book *Save The Cat* is worthless (the answer is "no"). They argue whether it's better to copyright a script or register it with the Writers Guild (the answer is "copyright it").

Mostly, they are well-meaning writers with varying degrees of success. So, I encourage you to check in with these people online. Get to know them. Like their posts, and discuss the writer's issues with them. Once you know who they are, you can set up a meeting to have coffee with them in person.

All these methods are available to writers in Los Angeles. That rules out some of these options for nonlocal writers. Even if you don't live in LA, you can meet with other like-minded writers on the internet. You have no excuse.

You should also meet with agents, managers, directors, producers, and even actors. You ultimately want to sell your script, and you're not likely to sell it to another writer. Actors, directors, producers, and agents can make that happen.

Networking with nonwriting industry people
At a certain level, actors and directors are all looking for a great screenplay. They're looking for significant parts and great stories to showcase their talents. You're a screenwriter. You could end up helping their career.

Where can you find these folks? On the MeetUp.com site, you'll find groups like LA Actors and Filmmakers, Entertainment Entrepreneurs and Performers, LA Neo-Noir Cinemasters, and Creativity Workshop (LA).

On LinkedIn, you can find the Film Job Board for Los Angeles, the Film Financing Group, Film and TV Professionals, Independent Filmmakers, and Actors and Casting Directors.

On Facebook, you can find the Indie Film Scene, Movieworld, the Independent Film Society, Cinema Discussions, Creative Designers and Writers, Film Industry Network, and Film and TV Professionals.

Networking at film festivals in LA

Another place where you might find actors, directors, and producers, in addition to writers, is at the various film festivals that take place in and around Los Angeles.

One of LA's best-known festivals is the Sundance Next Fest, which brings Sundance films to screen in LA. They hold screenings in downtown Los Angeles at the Ace Hotel Theater. Dances with Films is another film festival that takes place at TCL (formerly Grauman's) Chinese multiplex theater on Hollywood Boulevard.

For horror film fans, the Scream Fest runs for 10 days before Halloween at the Chinese theater. It's the most extensive and longest-running horror film festival in the country.

The AFI Film Festival screens at the Chinese and Egyptian theaters in Hollywood. One significant benefit of the AFI Film Festival is that it's free. You can join Film Independent. They sponsor the Independent Spirit Awards. Plus, they host more than 250 screenings every year.

Film schools also sponsor events that are open to the public. LA has some of the best film programs, including Loyola Marymount, Chapman, CalArts, AFI, UCLA, and USC. Check out their websites. You'll find events like mixers (Scripts, Wine & Chips) and screenings, like UCLA's Movies on the Green and Beachside Cinema.

Hopefully, you'll meet a director or a producer who likes your ideas. You might even find an agent. Remember, you don't ask for help when you first meet these people. You nurture relationships. Eventually, Karma kicks in, and all your hard work gets paid back.

CHAPTER 32

Find a Screenwriting Mentor

Finding a screenwriting mentor is a lot like networking. You have to figure out how to contact a potential mentor, establish a relationship, and nourish it. It takes a lot of effort. Unfortunately, you can't just buy them coffee and ask for a job. That's not the way it works.

Don't worry, you can do it.

If you're lucky, you know somebody who knows somebody who knows a screenwriter. Maybe your father sold a condo to a guy who writes for TV. Or that cousin who moved to Hollywood finally sold a screenplay. You're just a phone call away.

If you're not that lucky, though, you'll have to do some detective work. Try using LinkedIn or a Facebook writers' group. Try Google or the Internet Movie Database Pro (IMDB Pro). Find out if your mentor has an office on a studio lot. If they do, they'll have a phone number.

When trying to forge a relationship with a working writer, it might help to think about what you have in common. Did you go to the same college? Did you grow up in the same town? Maybe you were a member of the same club or sorority in college.

Maybe you both share some of the same interests? You can find out if your mentor gives to specific charities or if they are interested in race cars, fly fishing, collecting ceramic hedgehogs, or whatever. The more it feels like friendship and less like "What can you do for me?"—the better.

When you first reach out, try sending a letter or an email. Ask for a few minutes of their time on the phone. Schedule a phone call at a convenient time for them. Be familiar with their work. Tell them you love it—lie if you have to. Remember, you're trying to impress them.

Keep the conversation light. Be charming. Be interested.

If the first contact goes well, send a thank-you email. If you get the sense that you didn't freak them out, you might ask to meet for coffee at Starbucks. (Pick a Starbucks near them, not you.)

If they do agree to meet, show up prepared with specific questions. Ask about their career, "How did you break in?" "What writers inspired you?" "How did you find your agent?" Keep it short. Remember, they are doing you a favor.

At some point, you want to give them a writing sample. Make sure it's absolutely your best work. This all falls apart if your work is shoddy. If they agree, be prepared for the feedback and know it'll probably be critical. That's fine. You're going to need to know your weaknesses as well as your strengths.

Another great way to find a mentor is to take a class from an experienced professional.

Early in our careers, my partner, Steve Sustarsic, and I found mentors in Sam Locke and Lorenzo Music. Music co-created *The Bob Newhart Show* and *Rhoda*. Locke wrote for lots of shows, including *McHale's Navy* and *All in the Family*.

They both offered TV comedy writing classes. We wrote and honed our best TV writing samples—a *Taxi* and a *Barney Miller* spec—in their classes.

Why do I recommend classes? Two reasons:

1. We didn't have to call them to introduce ourselves.
2. We didn't have to ask them to read our scripts. It was the class assignment.

Fortunately, we were able to form relationships with these writers. We stayed in touch. They gave us lots of great advice over the years. We even occasionally collaborated with them.

At one point, Lorenzo Music approached us about collaborating on a TV pilot for Dom DeLuise. The three of us wrote up the pitch. It was so funny—too bad, though, because nobody bought it. It would have been great.

We were blessed to have these mentors in our lives.

I encourage you to find writing classes taught by established professionals. Just Google "screenwriting classes." You'll find plenty of them in LA. UCLA Extension has some taught by professionals. An organization called Master Class offers classes taught by writers like Shonda Rhimes and Mindy Kaling.

Hopefully, you'll find someone out there who's willing to help. One thing I've noticed is that it's generally easier to make contact with a professional writer who's retired. They have more time to spare and are probably bored to death.

SECTION 6

WHERE DO MOVIE IDEAS COME FROM?

CHAPTER 33

Look for Movie Ideas in the Public Domain

A*lice in Wonderland. Huckleberry Finn. Sherlock Holmes. The Invisible Man. Pride and Prejudice. Dracula. Tom Sawyer. Sense and Sensibility. The War of the Worlds.*

What do these movies have in common? They were all adapted from original source material under the rules of "public domain." Essentially, that means a screenwriter waited for the original copyrights to run out and then adapted these materials at no cost.

It's not a bad deal. These stories have been loved and admired by millions of readers over the years. They have a built-in appeal to a large audience. The films that were produced based on those scripts over the years have made millions of dollars.

Why do fans of these books and plays flock to the theaters? For one thing, they loved the experience of reading the originals and want to relive it. They might also want to see what filmmakers have done with the material. They want to know who will play the lead or the bad guy.

Understandably, actors are drawn to the material. Works by great authors are filled with juicy roles. Think of all the Oscars that have been earned over the years from adaptations of great literature. Directors go where the actors go. And with actors and directors attached, the studios can easily fund the projects.

If you decide to adapt a novel or play, you'll want to check with a lawyer. Copyright laws vary from country to country. In our country, copyright laws say you can use material without purchasing film rights 70 years after the author has died. Every year screenwriters mark their calendars, waiting for new titles to become available.

The laws aren't quite that simple. There are other ways a literary work can fall into the public domain. For example, works that are centuries old may have been written before copyright laws existed. In some instances, authors can decide if they want their work to be considered public domain.

While you can adapt the stories from these timeless novels and plays as they were written, there's another way to go. Consider retelling the stories in the current day or in a different environment.

Think about *West Side Story* (1961). The film, based on the classic story of star-crossed lovers *Romeo and Juliet*, was filmed by director Robert Wise and Jerome Robbins and was a massive hit in the early '60s, starring Natalie Wood. The film won 10 Academy Awards that year, including best film.

A favorite animated film, *The Lion King* (1994), was clearly inspired by *Hamlet*, a story in which the leadership of a Prince's kingdom is usurped by his evil Uncle, who kills his father and marries his mother to take power.

10 Things I Hate About You (1999) and *Deliver Us from Eva* (2003), two successful comedies, were based on the same Shakespeare play—*The Taming of the Shrew.*

Look for Movie Ideas in the Public Domain

10 Things I Hate About You was adapted for the screen by the writing team behind *Legally Blonde*, Karen McCullah Lutz and Kirsten Smith. The screenplay for *Deliver Us from Eva* was adapted by James Iver Mattson, B.E. Brauner, and Gary Hardwick.

She's the Man (2006) was successfully adapted from Shakespeare's *Twelfth Night*. In the film, Amanda Bynes poses as her brother to play on the high school soccer team. As in the play (posing as a boy), she gets involved "romantically" with another girl at school.

The movie *Cruel Intentions* (1999) was written by Roger Kumble and was based on the French novel *Les Liaisons Dangereuses*. The film was set in a present-day high school setting and starred Sarah Michelle Gellar, Reese Witherspoon, and Ryan Phillippe.

The list goes on, including *The Phantom of Paradise*, based on *The Phantom of the Opera*; *My Own Private Idaho*, based on Falstaff's subplots in *Henry IV* (Part 1), *Henry IV* (part 2), and *Henry V*; *Moulin Rouge!*, based in part on *La Boheme*; *My Fair Lady*, based on *Pygmalion*; and *A Knight's Tale*, based on *The Canterbury Tales*.

Some of the best screenwriters have adapted public domain stories. Don't feel like it's a cop-out. You'll be in good company. What's more, these days, Hollywood studios absolutely love to adapt existing "intellectual properties." They get built-in audiences and timeless material that appeals to the best actors and directors.

You might consider adapting stories like these—they won't cost you anything. And they may just get you discovered.

CHAPTER 34

Create a "Mash-up" of Two Stories

Here are a couple of examples of movie mash-ups: *Outland* is basically *High Noon*, with Sean Connery in the Gary Cooper role. It takes place on one of Jupiter's moons. *Alien* was pitched to the studios as *Jaws* in space by Ridley Scott. Both projects were created in the same way.

With *Outland* and *Alien*, the writers took successful films and made changes in the locale, the characters, and the time frame. Writers have been doing it forever. It's consistent with the idea that creativity is about synthesis—combining two concepts to create a new one.

Playing around with genre is another way. There are dozens of genres and subgenres. The most popular genres include drama, comedy, love stories, action, adventure, crime stories, westerns, war stories, horror, science fiction, and fantasy. Then there are sub-sub genres like survival horror and steampunk.

While some films fit neatly into one genre, say in the sense that *Tombstone* is a classic Western, consider *Blazing Saddles* and *A Million Ways to Die in the West*, both comedy-westerns.

Mel Brooks and Seth MacFarlane decided to take classic Western stories and make them into comedies, another way to come up with fresh ideas.

Some of the best romantic comedies involved a classic film subgenre, the "opposites attract love story." Lots of movie ideas came out of this notion of putting opposites together.

For example, Alvy Singer (played by Woody Allen), the "neurotic Jew," falls for the goyish Midwesterner Annie (played by Diane Keaton) in the Oscar-winning film *Annie Hall*.

In *As Good as It Gets*, Melvin (Jack Nicholson), a rude, crotchety, and wealthy romance novelist with OCD, hooks up with a sweet, loving, and painfully poor waitress, Carol (Helen Hunt).

The "opposites attract" theme has been a staple of romantic comedies going back to *It Happened One Night* and *Bringing Up Baby*. Think of a pair of opposites you haven't seen yet, and you may have found the germ of a new storyline.

Those dynamics have also worked well in character comedies, such as The *Odd Couple* (with Walter Matthau and Jack Lemmon) and *Grumpy Old Men* (also with Matthau and Lemmon).

You can see how writers have come up with ideas in the past by looking at existing storylines and then adding a twist. They think about ways to make a classic plot, theme, or genre fresh by changing it up—just enough.

Even the zombie movie *Warm Bodies* is a recent revision of *Romeo and Juliet*. In that movie, one of the star-crossed lovers is a zombie, and the other is a living human. Talk about an odd couple.

Writers have created lots of hit movies by adding zombies to classic stories. *World War Z*, for example, combines a war genre with a horror-zombie subgenre. *Shaun of the Dead* and *Evil Dead 2* combine zombies with comedic storylines.

Screenwriters have been using this method for years to develop script ideas. One writer created a fresh approach by telling the story of Abraham Lincoln but by adding vampires in the historical spoof *Abraham Lincoln Vampire Killer*.

Quentin Tarantino and Robert Rodriguez came up with a fresh idea by combining a straight-up crime drama with a horror-vampire film—in *Dusk Till Dawn*.

James Cameron came up with a great twist on the disaster film with his classic movie *Titanic*. He combined the disaster film with the coming-of-age love story between Rose DeWitt (Kate Winslet) and Jack Dawson (Leonardo DiCaprio).

Dances With Wolves, starring Kevin Costner, was another very successful combination of film genres: the classic fish-out-of-water genre and the western. Costner's character is a Caucasian soldier who is wounded, near death, and falls on hard times. He accepts the native culture and eventually lives with and adopts the ways of his sworn enemy, the Lakota Sioux.

James Cameron decided to take the *Dances With Wolves* story, push it into the future, and add aliens. Again, he successfully combined various genres and came up with a hit film. *Avatar* is still one of the highest-grossing films of all time.

Many great film ideas have come from looking at two or more successful films and combining elements of each. When thinking of ideas for your next screenplay, you might try playing around with existing plots and genres.

Some other examples: in writing *Django, Unchained*, Tarantino combined a civil war era western with a samurai movie. *Blade Runner* was a sci-fi story told against a film noir background. Kubrick took an action-adventure tale about nuclear war (*Fail Safe*), turned it on its head, and came up with *Dr. Strangelove*, a dark comedy satirizing our fascination with nukes.

Think about the movies you've seen. Look at all the films on Netflix or Amazon Prime. Imagine what the film would be like with gay characters instead of straight; imagine if it took place on another planet or in the Middle Ages and had a mythic quality. Of course, you will need to make it your own; you can't keep all the elements. Be creative and put your stamp on it. Write it in your distinctive voice.

CHAPTER 35

Adapting Books and Plays

The Godfather. Terms of Endearment. Fear and Loathing in Las Vegas. Casablanca. On the Waterfront. Chicago. Harry Potter. The Exorcist. Nomadland.

What do they all have in common? They were all adapted from successful novels or plays. Some of them won Oscars. A couple of them spawned sequels and prequels. All these films made a fortune at the box office. The studios love to buy projects like these.

Let's look at an example. *One Flew Over the Cuckoo's Nest* started as a novel written by Ken Kesey in 1962. Kesey wrote about his experiences and observations working in and around a mental hospital in Palo Alto, California. The novel was later adapted into a stage play by Dale Wasserman. It was a big hit on Broadway, where McMurphy was played by Gary Sinise, and later Kirk Douglas.

Douglas bought the film rights to the novel from Ken Kesey for $20,000. That's right, $20,000. Laurence Hauben and Bo Goldman wrote a screenplay based on the novel. After a while, Douglas gave the rights to his son, Michael Douglas, who decided to produce the film. Kirk Douglas was too old to play McMurphy by that time, so Jack Nicholson got the role.

The movie came out in 1975. The movie, directed by Milos Forman, was the second film ever to sweep the five major categories at the Academy Awards—Best Picture, Best Director, Best Screenplay, Best Actor, and Best Actress.

Let's say you find a novel or a play you think would make a great movie. How do you option or buy the film rights? Typically, the producer secures the rights. Writers can do it, too.

You have to figure out who owns the rights. The best place to start is to contact the writer. Verify that the writer of the novel or play does, in fact, hold the rights. Be sure it's not the publisher, as sometimes happens. If the rights are available, talk with the writer about making a deal to option or buy them.

How much should you pay for the rights? The original writer might be expecting a big payday. Studios have been known to pay $10,000 or more for these kinds of options. Since you're just starting out, let's assume you can't afford that kind of money.

You'll want to look for books and plays with modest success. You can't afford books on the bestseller list. Look for material that did moderately well but still got excellent reviews.

If your budget is limited, talk to the writer about how a movie based on their work would boost their book sales. You might even get them to option their work for a minimal fee. Dollar options do happen.

Salesmanship helps. You might be thinking, "Wait a minute here, I'm a writer, not a salesman. Isn't that what

Adapting Books and Plays

agents are for?" Well, when you're starting out, you kind of have to be your own agent. Sorry, but that's the reality.

Most writers don't actually buy the film rights, they option them. What does this mean? It means you set out a contract with the original writer to hold the exclusive rights for a year or two while you write the adaptation and try to sell it. During that period, no one else can adapt the material or shop it.

Part of your option contract sets out how much the original writer will make if you sell your script. How do you decide how much you'll pay them? Probably best to say something like 20% of what you make.

As a first-time screenwriter, you won't make much money to share with them. You'll be lucky to make between $50,000 and $150,000 if you sell the script to a WGA signatory production company. Less if you sell to a low-budget producer.

You'll definitely want to get an entertainment lawyer involved. Issues like merchandising, residuals, and sequel rights will be involved. Tempers can flare when it comes to splitting profits. Play it safe. Hire a lawyer.

Another approach is to partner with the original writer on the screenplay. A couple of times, I've offered novelists a 50-50 split—meaning we would equally share the profits and the screen credit. We then wrote the script together. It's a very appealing offer for novelists. They all want movies made from their books. And if it works out, you'll both get paid, and both get credit.

A few years ago, writer-director Dan Mirvish found an off-Broadway play called *Between Us* that he thought would make a great low-budget film. There were only four main characters and just a few locations. There were significant parts for actors. It had the flavor of *Who's Afraid of Virginia Wolf?*

Mirvish approached the playwright Joe Hortua about adapting his play. Both writers collaborated on the screenplay. They shopped it around. Ultimately, Taye Diggs and Julia Stiles signed on. The film was greenlit in 2012.

When you option the rights to a project like this, you must think and act like a producer. If you can get the rights to a great book or play, you will help yourself in many ways. You'll potentially get a built-in buzz, positive reviews, a pre-sold audience, and material that will attract star talent. What have you got to lose?

CHAPTER 36
Adapting Newspaper or Magazine Articles

True stories are a great place to look for movie ideas. Unlike books and plays, newspaper and magazine articles don't generally get the attention of big-time producers like Scott Rudin or Jerry Bruckheimer. If you find a piece that you think will make a great film, you have a chance of getting the rights.

Fortunately for the screenwriters who wrote the following films, the articles they found were not huge bestsellers or Pulitzer Prize winners, nor were they well known. They were affordable. That's what you're looking for. Great story. Low profile.

- *Almost Famous*, based on the 1973 *Rolling Stone* article "The Allman Brothers" written by a teenage Cameron Crowe
- *Argo*, based on the article "How the CIA Used a Fake Sci-Fi Flick to Rescue Americans From Tehran," written by Joshua Bearman for *Wired Magazine*
- *The Fast and the Furious*, based on the 1998 *Vibe Magazine* article "Racer X," written by Kenneth Rafael

- *The Killing Fields*, based on the *New York Times* article "The Life and Death of Dith Pran," written by Sydney H. Schanberg
- *Boogie Nights*, based on the 1989 article "The Devil and John Holmes," written by Mike Sagers for *The Rolling Stone*
- *The Bling Ring*, originally a *Vanity Fair* article by Nancy Jo Sales titled "The Suspects Wore Louboutins."
- *The Dallas Buyers Club* told the story of how a homophobic cowboy with AIDS smuggled HIV drugs from Mexico (where they were legal) to Dallas (where they were definitely not permitted). *The Dallas Buyer's Club* is an excellent example of how you can find a news article that inspires you to write a great screenplay. And the author paid nothing for the film rights. Nothing!

How did the screenwriter Craig Borten find the article "Buying Time" in the *Dallas Morning News*, and how did he go from there to write an Academy Award-nominated screenplay?

The journey starts with Bill Minutaglio, a Texas journalist, who read an article in *The Village Voice* about smuggling HIV drugs from Mexico, which mentioned Ron Woodruff, a cowboy who was allegedly involved.

The Village Voice article explained that some very smart smugglers found a loophole in the law. Since selling the AIDS drugs outright was illegal, they created "buyers clubs," which people joined for a fee or paid for with monthly dues, which gave them access to the drugs.

Minutaglio researched the phenomenon in the 1960s and wrote an article in the *Dallas Morning News* called "Buying Time."

Screenwriter Craig Borden found Minutaglio's story and realized it could spawn a great film. He saw Ron Woodruff and did a series of interviews with him over three days. In all, Borten completed 20 hours' worth of interviews.

In Borten's screenplay, the main character (Woodruff) changes through conflict, developing friendships with his HIV-positive customers and even a transgender HIV-positive character (played by Jared Leto in the film). He eventually becomes less self-involved and a bit of a hero.

Borten had enough for a story and based it on his interviews with Woodruff. He didn't exactly base it on the *Buying Time* newspaper article, so he never had to buy the film rights.

He wrote the screenplay and started showing it around. It was sold for the first time in 1996. At that point, Woody Harrelson was set to play Woodruff, and Dennis Hopper was set to direct.

The company that bought the script, however, eventually went bankrupt. Later, Borten rewrote the script with Melisa Wallack, and, in 1997, they sold it to Universal. They wanted Brad Pitt to play Woodruff and Marc Foster (director of *Monster's Ball*) to direct. However, Pitt decided to make *World War Z* instead. The deal fell apart.

The screenplay sat on a shelf for about ten years. Then, due to an overlooked clause in their Writer's Guild contract, Borten and Wallack were able to get the film rights back. Eventually, the film was made.

Dallas Buyer's Club won Academy Awards for best actor (McConaughey) and best supporting actor (Jared Leto). The writers, Borten and Wallack, were nominated for an Academy Award for best screenplay.

Real life doesn't always fit nicely into the three-act structure. The true story may involve too many or too few characters for a screen story. You may have to take a dramatic license when you adapt these articles.

Borten and Wallack certainly took liberties in *Dallas Buyer's Club*. The transsexual character played by Jared Leo and the doctor played by Jennifer Garner, for example, were composites. Those characters didn't really exist.

Just as with novels and plays, you'll have to think like a producer to secure the rights to an article. This involves finding out who actually owns the rights to the piece. Remember, sometimes it's the publisher. The rights could be shared. Be careful. Negotiate a fair deal. And always use a lawyer.

Look out for articles that catch your interest. Who knows where a great idea will come from? We are living in interesting times, maybe too interesting. There's no such thing as a slow news day anymore. Keep an eye out. You just might find the idea for your next script.

SECTION 7

HOW TO SELL YOUR SCREENPLAY

CHAPTER 37

Selling Your First Script

Finishing your first screenplay is a very big deal. Lots of beginning writers start writing them, then get hung up somewhere along the way. If you have actually finished a screenplay, congratulations! Pat yourself on the back. Now what?

Now, you have to think about how to sell it. You have to sell these things after you write them. Otherwise, it's just a hobby. The truth is that most aspiring screenwriters haven't got a clue about selling scripts.

I think most writers consider themselves "artists." Like all artists since the beginning of time, they think they'll get "discovered." They figure if their scripts are good enough, the word will get out. That's kind of what I thought.

Nobody teaches you how to sell your scripts. I didn't learn how to do it at the Learning Annex or USC. None of those books I bought about screenwriting helped, either. I guess I didn't give it a lot of thought.

I just assumed I would eventually get an agent, and they would sell my scripts. I didn't realize that getting an agent is not that easy. There's a Catch-22. It goes like this: you need an agent to sell your script. And an agent won't sign you unless you've already sold a script. It's been like this forever.

So, how do you sell a screenplay?

When I started, I didn't know the answer to that question. My partner, Steve Sustarsic, and I tried however we could to get our scripts out there. We got jobs as production assistants at Mace Neufeld Productions, and I got a job doing script coverage for American International Pictures. We kept our sample spec scripts in the car in case we met a producer.

Everywhere we went, we were ready to hand out a script. We were opportunists. We mailed them to producers (that's right, snail mail). We always included a signed release form.

There's a reason producers won't read scripts not sent by an agent. They're afraid of getting sued for stealing the material. If they read a script and then, years later, produce a film with a similar story, they could get sued. They need to be protected.

When material is sent by agents, they are absolved of that liability. That's also the purpose of a signed release form.

Sign the release forms. My partner and I wrote a couple of really good spec TV scripts, which we sent to writers and producers with the signed release forms.

Years before, Steve had sent a script to a writer named Tom Tenowich. He wasn't the showrunner, but his name appeared on the credits somewhere, so Steve chose him–less pressure, he figured, than sending it to the head writer.

At that time, he couldn't help much.

Fortunately, when we sent him our latest spec scripts, he liked them both. A lot. Enough to invite us to pitch the show he was producing, *Mork and Mindy*. No pressure. It was only, like, the number one show on television. It was the first show we pitched.

We sold them a story.

Tenowich and another producer on that show, Ed Scharlach, talked with producers on other shows about how much they liked our work. We didn't ask them to; they just did it. (We were really lucky.)

Jay Moriarty, on *The Jeffersons,* asked Scharlach about up-and-coming writers. Scharlach mentioned our names. Moriarty and his partner, Mike Milligan, had us come in to pitch stories for their show.

In a short time, we sold an episode to *The Jeffersons.* They liked the job we did. They invited us back.

I always kept our spec scripts (with release forms) with me. After a meeting at *The Jeffersons*, I literally walked down the hall and dropped our specs (with releases) on the desk of a story editor at *One Day at a Time.*

A week later, he called us. We were invited to pitch there, too. The producers at that show said, "When we find writers who can write, we hire them." So, that's how we got our first staff jobs—as story editors. Within a few weeks, we had dropped our scripts off on the story editor's desk and then were hired for his job, as he moved up to producer.

We were now working writers. From that point on, we had agents. However, that didn't mean we could stop selling ourselves. We never stopped making contacts, meeting with other agents, writing new spec scripts, and reinventing ourselves.

That's how it works, especially in the beginning. Once we had an agent, they started finding us work.

CHAPTER 38

What to Do After Finishing Your First Draft

What do you do when you've finished your first draft? First, celebrate with someone close to you who understands how important it is. Take time to reflect on what you've accomplished. Then, take a break.

Put the script away and come up with some other ideas for screenplays. Having lots of ideas in various stages of development bulletproofs you from rejection. If they don't like the script you submit, you have many others. What do you do next?

Copyright Your First Draft

You've got to be careful who you tell about the project. You don't want to get ripped off. One way to protect your script is to register it with the Writers Guild of America for between $10 and $20. You can do it online at www.wgawregistry.org.

However, a copyright is far superior. The WGA registration only lasts for five years, whereas copyrights last for the life of the writer plus 70 years.

How do you copyright your script?

It's best to do it online. You go to the Copyright Office Electronic System online, where you'll complete an application. You pay a small fee; you submit your work and then wait for your script to be copyrighted. The process will take several months.

Your script will change after this first draft as you incorporate feedback. You'll also want to copyright some of the next few drafts. Always copyright the final draft.

Keep in mind that you have to *kind of* trust people in this business. To sell a project, you have to pitch it. You have to give the script to other people to read. You have to get used to talking about your project when selling it.

Ideas do get stolen, but it doesn't happen all the time. You have to be able to live with risks. Hundreds of people will probably read your script before someone buys it.

Move on to the Second and Third Drafts, Then Prepare for Feedback

Take your time with the next draft and subsequent drafts. Whereas you could write almost stream-of-consciousness in your first draft, you will need to be more focused and deliberate.

Get your script to the point where you can't think of ways to improve it. Now, other people have to read it. You've got to prepare for feedback. Put yourself in a frame of mind to accept constructive criticism. Nobody likes this part.

People will be judging your script. Just remember, it's the script. They're only critiquing the writing. It's not you. And remember, you can get 1,000 "nos," but it only takes one "yes."

Ask a Trusted Friend Who Is Also a Writer to Read Your Work

Your friends will generally say good things. This is a safe way to start showing your work. Eventually, you want to show it to a more advanced writer. There are lots of them on social media. You want to listen to their critiques.

Your writer friends and more advanced writers will often be good at finding problems with your script. Take their criticism seriously. If several friends give you the same feedback, they probably are right.

Some people do table reads, using actors to read the parts out loud. Table reads are very helpful. You can tell if scenes fall flat, if you need some cuts, and where clarification might be necessary. The actors who read for you may have valuable input, too. There are writing groups in LA that hold table reads for their members. They may charge $30 a month, but it's worth it.

There's a website called Deadline Junkies Screenwriter's Lab that also offers table reads for writers. Their membership fees are reasonable. They not only have professional actors read your script, but professional writers will give you feedback.

Compare the Various Critiques

Look at all the feedback you've gotten, then decide what needs to be fixed. Be tough with yourself. The marketplace will be unforgiving. Try to remain objective, and remember, your career is about writing many screenplays on spec. If this one doesn't sell, it may be the one that gets you a pitch session. Figure out the most important fixes, then incorporate them into your next draft.

If you can afford it, this is a good time to send this more polished script to a professional story analyst.

I used to send my drafts to a writer who screened scripts for the Sundance Labs. I remember paying him $250 to evaluate and give feedback. He always let me tape-record our sessions, which helped with the next rewrite.

I know, you're saying, "Ack. More rewrites!" Sorry, but you'll have to get used to it. Even produced writers won't turn a script in without getting professional-level feedback. They always go the extra mile to get it right.

Incorporate the New Changes into Your Screenplay

You don't have to listen to everyone, but if there's a consensus, you'd be wise to pay attention. It's important to get it right. Your screenplay is like a calling card. Think of it as the script that kicks off your career.

CHAPTER 39

Ways to Get Your Script Read

If you have an agent or a manager, you'll want to strategize with them about where to send your screenplay. Most unproduced writers, however, don't have an agent or a manager. How do they get their script to the right people?

In many cases, it's all about finding contact information for actors, producers and directors, assistant directors, production managers, and the rest. You can use Google, Hollywood Directories, and the Internet Movie Data Base (IMDb).

Send Your Script to a Producer

Get your script directly to an actor, director, or producer. Believe it or not, some writers have managed to get their scripts directly into the hands of a person who can greenlight their film. How do you do this? It helps if you know somebody—a contact, a colleague, or a cousin who produces films.

Without an agent, you'll have to make it happen yourself. It takes a lot of nerve. If you're lucky, you might work on a studio lot and have access to actors, directors, or producers.

You'll have to move out of your comfort zone. Some people are lucky and can get a script to William Macy, or they know a guy who knows a guy who knows Kevin Bacon. It helps to be "connected."

Contests, Workshops, and Labs

The Academy Nicholl Fellowship is the best contest. It is sponsored by the Academy of Motion Picture Arts and Sciences. The next best are Austin and Page. Film festivals have contests. Some websites, like the Blacklist or Inktip, may also have competitions. If you place in the top 10%, or still better, win—you can add that to your query letter.

Sundance, Slamdance, and other festivals also have workshops. If your script makes the cut, they could have you come in to do their "lab" to rework or eventually shoot a scene.

Moviebytes lists hundreds of screenwriting contests. Before entering, ensure you get coverage from a reliable source, and make sure the script gets a RECOMMEND evaluation or a CONSIDER, at the very least. If it doesn't, you'll need to rewrite it. Other sources for coverage include The Blacklist and professionals who consult on scripts, like Erik Bork (writer of the Emmy-winning HBO series *Band of Brothers*).

The better the feedback you get, the better your rewrites will be. If you can afford to get feedback from someone like Erik Bork or another professional writer, your final product will show it. You might even consider a company like Greenlight Coverage, which is supposed to give you quality feedback using artificial intelligence. Disclaimer: I've never tried it, but they advertise that many writers using their service have sold their screenplays.

Warner and Disney offer internships. If accepted, they'll work with you on polishing your script or writing a new script in a workshop setting. Some of these are actually fellowships, which means the network or studio may pay you (up to $30,000 a year) to nurture you as a writer.

Also, as previously mentioned, many networks and studios have internships for writers who qualify as "diverse." This includes minorities, women, writers with disabilities, and writers over 55.

You can post your script on internet sites where producers, managers, and agents can access them.

Inktip (inktip.com) is one of the first websites to post written material for industry people to find. It has some success stories. There is a monthly fee, but it's not a rip-off. They will also list your logline in a brochure that's sent to 5,000 production companies.

The Blacklist (blacklst.com) is one of the best newer services to offer this type of exposure. They charge $25 per month to post your material. They also provide evaluations for screenplays and TV scripts at reasonable prices. Additionally, they offer contests and mentorship programs.

Some resources you can use to reach producers once your script is in great shape include Screenwriters Online, a website that will enable you to chat with a producer and participate in online pitch festivals like the one *FadeIn Magazine* (online) offers. Scriptshark promises to blast your script to hundreds of producers.

The International Screenwriting Association website advertises "Gigs." Most of these jobs are non-WGA writing jobs, so take advantage of them while you're working your way up and before you're in the guild.

You can also blog about your writing "adventures" online. Allegedly, Diablo Cody (*Juno, Young Adult*) was "discovered" based on her blog about working as a stripper while breaking in. Some people set up Facebook "Like" pages for their projects. Some people create websites to promote their material.

Shoot a Short Film

Writers who are also directors have a better shot at breaking into the film industry. They can write and make a short film that gets them noticed. For example, *Sling Blade* (Billy Bob Thorton), *Frankenweenie* (Tim Burton), and *Bottle Rocket* (Wes Anderson) were all features made from shorts.

If you can direct and write, you might shoot your best scene and put it on your website. Even better, put together a "sizzle reel" featuring 10-20 quick highlights from the film edited together. Then use social media, Twitter, LinkedIn, and Facebook to make sure people see it.

"Has-Beens" and "Up-and-Comers"

Send your script to talented, ambitious "up-and-comers." Find addresses, emails, or phone numbers for up-and-coming commercial directors, music video directors, assistant directors, cinematographers, production managers, and even casting directors.

These people don't want to stay where they are. Everybody wants to be a filmmaker, so they are motivated to read your script, which may help them break through.

Consider sending scripts to "has-been" actors—former stars still looking for significant parts. They may still be bankable and generally have the right contacts. They know producers, directors, and other actors. If they love your script, they have lots of leverage. Don't call them has-beens.

These are just suggestions. You don't have to try any or all of these. Look at your budget. Entering contests, workshops, and labs, as well as subscribing to IMDb Pro costs money. Getting a professional to give you feedback costs money. Ask yourself what makes the most sense to you and what you can afford.

A lot of screenwriters, especially first-time writers, don't feel like they can afford anything. A word of caution. In almost all careers, you spend money to succeed. Either you go to college, take courses, advertise, or network. Screenwriting is the same. Five hundred dollars may seem like a lot to pay a script consultant like Erik Bork. Think about it this way—it's your dream. You have to invest in yourself.

CHAPTER 40

Write for the Gatekeepers

When I started writing coverage for a studio, I had no idea how demanding a job it would be. I'd written some coverage in film classes, but I had plenty of time to read the script, assess its strengths and weaknesses, and write it all up in a nice, concise package. I could take a few days to write it.

Once I was on the job, I learned that you have to read a new script every day—sometimes a new novel every day. You don't have time to pore over the material and soak it up. You have just a few hours to read the material, summarize it, write an assessment—*and* proof everything.

The hardest part of the process for me was summarizing a screenplay's story while conveying a sense of the characters, the plot, the dialogue, the tone, and the pace of the script. Try to describe 115 pages of romance, jokes, suspense, or what-have-you in half a page. It was not easy.

Additionally, you must make a convincing argument as to why the story, plot, characters, and pace either work or fall short. You also have to back up your opinions with evidence. If you say the script has weak dialogue or poor story structure, you need to back it up with examples.

Pass/Consider/Recommend

You have to decide whether to pass, consider, or recommend the script to the studio executives. If you recommend a screenplay, then your coverage gets noticed by the people upstairs. Everybody will read the script, and if they all hate it, well, that's on you.

As a result, you want to save your praise for only the very best scripts. You don't want to go to bat for a so-so or even a decent script with flaws. I always felt like my job was on the line if I recommended a script.

After reading scripts for a living, you get a feel for what works and what doesn't. Some readers will tell you they know, in the first 10 pages, whether they will pass on a script.

How Do You Get Past the "Gatekeepers"?

What do the story analysts look for? What do you have to do to get a "consider" or maybe even a "recommend?"

From my time reading and mostly passing on scripts, here are some pointers. However, first, a disclaimer: there are no absolute rules in Hollywood. These are just guidelines:

- Be sure the first 10 pages grab the reader's attention. Avoid clichéd, slow, hackneyed openings. Never be boring.
- Make sure all the major characters have distinctive, three-dimensional personalities. Let them act and talk believably. The main character grows through conflict. Minor characters have arcs, too.
- Don't write overly long (seven- or eight-page) scenes with talking heads and little action. It's a movie—a motion picture. The average scene is about two pages.

Average—meaning you'll have some half-page and three- or four-page scenes. You can have 10-page scenes, but you want an average of about two.

- Don't write seven-to-10-line, single-space descriptions of action. You want to make sure there is maximum white space. Don't write long blocks of dialogue, either. Keep the dialogue conversational.
- Do not write scenes that don't forward the story or a subplot. You can tell if it doesn't. If you cut the scene, will the story still progress without it? If so, cut away.
- Know when to get into a scene and when to get out. Write every scene with a beginning, middle, and end, or at least a middle and an end. Try to build to a funny, scary, or otherwise entertaining payoff, then get out of the scene.
- Avoid obvious exposition.
- Don't write scenes where characters talk about another character without moving the story. If you must push information, make it part of a scene that moves the story forward. Make sure there's conflict in the scene.
- Be careful with voice-overs. If you use them, make sure they don't just reiterate the action or state information without being entertaining.
- Don't mess with the margins to control your page count. Write a script that's between 90 to 120 pages. When in doubt, cut.
- Your main story and subplots almost always start early in Act One and progress into Act Three. You

want them to build to a climax around two-thirds of the way through.

- Don't submit a script full of typos, misspellings, awkward grammar, run-on sentences, or annoying, gross, or obscene dialogue—unless there's a very good reason for it.
- Don't introduce 10 characters in the same scene. Make it easy for the reader to keep track of who's who. Don't create characters with names that sound alike.
- Be careful not to use too many flashbacks or flashforwards. Be clear about the timeline, and don't confuse the reader; don't make them go back and try to figure it out.
- When we first see the character, write their first and last names in capital letters, with their age, something about their look, and a hint about their personality or attitude.
- When you write witty or funny dialogue, avoid corny jokes, puns, stupid jokes, jokes that would prompt a rim-shot, and dated references. Funny dialogue should sound conversational and not have a setup-joke rhythm.
- End on a high note.
- Come up with a thoughtful, satisfying, and, hopefully, unexpected ending. Complete the main character's arc in a satisfying way. Try to move the reader. Look for emotional endings. Set them up. Earn them.
- Don't write female characters that are merely sexy or pretty. It's okay if they're attractive, but there should be

more going on. Note: there are a lot of women in the story departments at the studios. Don't piss them off.
- The "Bechtel test." You should at least be familiar with it. The test posits this rule: You need at least two female characters in the movie who talk to each other. They have to talk about something other than a male.
- Make sure the stakes are high for your protagonist. The stakes supply motivation and urgency. Without that urgency, your story won't be a quick read—it'll feel sluggish.
- Your hero will need setbacks, and they should get tougher as the story unfolds. Don't forget to place obstacles in their way. The obstacles grow in intensity, building to the climax. Don't forget the third act has a structure. Act Three has its own setbacks and obstacles.

The general idea is to make it easy for the story analyst to get through your script. All the screenplays I recommended were real page-turners.

CHAPTER 41

How to Get an Agent or a Manager

One way of getting an agent or manager is to sell a screenplay. Agents have a sixth sense about screenplay sales. Once you've sold one, they'll come out of the woodwork to close your deal and, of course, take their commission. Yes, they will take their 10 percent on your first sale, even though you're the one who made it happen. There are no freebies.

It's important to let the agent close your deal. If you sell a feature screenplay or TV script, agents will happily close the deal and take their 10 percent. If you sell a script and keep every penny, agents may still want to rep you, but it's less likely.

If you're not lucky enough to make a sale, you'll need to submit your scripts to various representatives and hope they like your material. Unfortunately, with fewer screenplays selling each year, agents are scratching and clawing just to get their established writer's work. They don't have time to grow "baby writers."

Breaking new writers is tougher than it's ever been. Agents want to make money. They prioritize finding work for their best writers. That's how they make the big bucks.

Managers Versus Agents

Managers are different.

What's the difference? Speaking generally, while agents limit their activities to "fielding offers," packaging projects, and closing deals, managers are known for growing screenwriters. Both will give you notes on your screenplay. The manager will be more likely to sit down with you and help you fix it.

Another difference is that an agent works for an agency. They might represent 30 to 50 writers. Managers tend to have fewer, with an average of around 20. Agents are limited to taking a 10% commission, while managers usually take 15%.

Managers also want to produce films, which can be a plus. They may actually produce your script. However, sometimes their priority is more about production than selling scripts. They can make a lot more as producers.

My advice is to sign with a manager. Managers will be more patient with you while you are still finding your voice. They're more willing to nurture new talent—up to a point.

Keep in mind that both agents and managers will only be so patient with you. Their time is valuable. If you're not selling scripts, getting TV staff positions, or improving as a writer, be warned—they will pull the plug.

What are they looking for?

They're looking for screenplays that sell. They're looking for writers who are writing at a professional level. Your first few screenplays will probably not make the cut. If you don't get a manager based on your first effort, be patient.

Both agents and managers are looking for writers who understand the market, have a commercial sensibility, and are committed to their craft. They don't want to nurture a baby writer for a year only to have them give up when the going gets tough.

Screenwriting representatives are also looking for writers who are comfortable in a room and who know how to pitch and talk story in meetings with producers. A writer who's good on paper but freezes up in meetings can have a short career.

How do you get your script to the representative? First, make sure you're sending out a fantastic screenplay or teleplay. You want to blow their minds. Don't send out an average script; be sure it's polished and proofed.

Then, you'll need to get emails for the representatives. Check out *The Hollywood Creative Directory.* Then, you need to write a query letter.

About the Query Letter

You want to write a letter directly to the agent or manager. Try to get their name. The key to the query letter is the logline. Keep the message brief. After their address, and "Dear So-and-So," put the logline at the top of your letter.

Start with a brief statement, "Please consider my feature-length screenplay, *The XYZ Story.*" Quick and to the point.

Next, include your logline. What does a great logline look like? Here's one for the movie *The Exorcist*: When an innocent twelve-year-old girl is mysteriously possessed by a demon, her mother enlists the aid of a Catholic priest, who stands up to the devil himself to save her daughter's soul.

We learn who the characters are, their goals, and the obstacles that stand in their way. A girl's soul lies in the balance. The stakes are high.

A good logline is supposed to be short—some say less than 35 words. That's a good rule of thumb. The truth is, nobody will be counting. You can go over. You can use two sentences.

Next, you mention that you're a produced screenwriter and list your recent credits. If you're not produced, cite other accomplishments, like placing fourth in the Page Screenwriting competition. Don't write a long autobiography. Keep it simple.

Then finish with something like, "Please let me know if I can send you the full screenplay, and I'll send it immediately." Mention that you'll include a signed release form with the script. Thank them for their consideration.

Hopefully, you'll sell a screenplay, and agents will come to you. In the next best scenario, you'll get a manager who will help you grow as a writer. Who knows, maybe you'll wind up getting both an agent *and* a manager.

You'll double your chances of selling, but you'll be parting with 25 percent of your paycheck. In my opinion, it's worth it.

SECTION 8

SURVIVING HOLLYWOOD

CHAPTER 42

What Is a Writer's Personality?

Most writers won't need the advice in these last few chapters, but for those who do, here's my input as a screenwriter, who also happens to be a psychotherapist.

While all writers are not the same, you could say some common themes run through their lives. They tend to be bright, driven, accomplished people with a high degree of sensitivity.

Writing involves constructing unforgettable characters. Writers tend to be students of human behavior. They have a remarkable ability to empathize with others, and they need to empathize with the characters they create.

While most writers I know are on the shy side, they also have to promote themselves. They have to break out of their shells to meet people. Some of the writers I've known have actually been somewhat socially awkward. They tended to have trouble with networking and pitching.

Are writers introverted?

Shyness and being introverted are not exactly the same. Shy people tend to feel anxious around strangers or when facing large groups. It's about how they deal with social situations. Introverts, in contrast, tend to be more involved in their inner world.

Writers have the ability to spend long periods inside their heads. They work from the inside out. Extroverts are the other way around. Extroverts are creative, too—they just do better around other people.

People think of introverts as quiet, well-mannered people. Some people consider themselves introverted, yet can open up and even appear extroverted at times. I've known writers like that, too. It's like flipping a switch.

Another thing about these folks. They tend to be overanalytical. Writing is all about attention to detail. You might think of a writer who's "anguished over his story." They stress out over the choices. What would their characters do? What's the most interesting choice?

A writing career can be extremely stressful. All that time working in isolation can take a toll. You've heard about writers who famously "suffered" for their art. Part of being a writer involves being severely critical of one's work.

They face constant judgment and rejection almost throughout their entire careers. When they finally succeed, critics will say, "So you did it once; you wrote a film that became a hit—that's the Holy Grail of Hollywood." A few months later, they'll say, "What have you done lately."

You've probably noticed that many famous writers have used alcohol and drugs as a crutch to get them through their stressed-out lives.

Earlier, we talked about writers like Aaron Sorkin, Stephen King, and Philip K. Dick, who drank or used hard drugs to get through their scripts. They found substances

What Is a Writer's Personality?

like coke or amphetamines to keep them writing. They self-medicated to endure the deluge of self-criticism.

Writers have got to be strong. They have to learn to live in moderation. Those drugs, those uppers, those downers, that booze: it can get you through short-term, but they cause damage long term, especially to sensitive people.

While not all writers have the same personality traits, they share some common characteristics. Writers spend long, difficult hours in isolation, writing and rewriting endlessly. The odds are very steep. Yet, they persevere.

Surviving in this town can come at a price. Remember to take care of yourself.

CHAPTER 43

Surviving Social Anxiety in Hollywood

Do you have problems pitching to producers? Do you feel your heart racing? Do you stutter or "freeze up" in front of a group? Do you get tense meeting strangers? Do you have a hard time working the room at a party? Believe me, I've been there.

I believe the source of all social anxiety goes back to a fear of being judged. When I feel that people are judging me or my performance, I can suddenly think of a million reasons why they're right.

Much of the time, we just *assume* people are judging us. We don't know *for sure,* but we imagine the worst. Why does that happen? Psychologists call it a "negativity bias." Our brains are always preparing for the worst-case scenario.

I've had lots of great experiences pitching movie and pilot ideas, and I've sold a fair number of them. I've somehow managed to co-create a few TV shows. When it comes time to do it again, I suddenly forget all that. It never fails.

How to Successfully Pitch

How do you avoid freezing up at a pitch? First, don't forget to breathe. Before going into the meeting, take a few deep breaths. Try "yoga breathing." Inhale through your nose and exhale slowly through your mouth. Learn how to center yourself.

Think rationally

You've given successful presentations but still "freeze up" when faced with a new one. Why does your mind go there? It's that "negativity bias." We go there because fear takes over.

Think logically, without fear. Don't let past rejections get to you. Remember, you have done this before, and it didn't kill you. You'll live. Take a deep breath, do what you can to relax, and look at the situation rationally. Focus on your successes. Be confident.

Show up prepared

Don't show up for a networking event without something to say. If you don't prepare, you'll be nervous, and you'll wait for somebody else to make the first move. When you're waiting like that, you won't feel in control.

Come prepared with an interesting story, some news, or even some gossip. Now you have something to talk about. Go right up to somebody and start a conversation. Rip off the Band-Aid. Everything that follows gets easier.

If you still get rattled at parties, you might try using a prop. Bring your phone with photos of your dog, your girlfriend, your vacation pictures, whatever. Show them around. Talk about the dog. I find it's easier to tell a story when people aren't staring at me.

The same thing applies to speeches. They make me nervous. I'll bring a visual aid, like a chart or PowerPoint presentation. That way, I can point to the screen the whole time. When all eyes are on me, it's not good—I freeze up.

Exposure therapy

If you struggle with social anxiety, you can try exposure therapy. You should probably contact a therapist about this. The idea is that you expose yourself to social situations—a little at a time. Set manageable goals. Start with something easy. Ask a stranger for directions. There's not a lot at stake. Work up to more challenging situations slowly.

Every time you take steps outside your comfort zone, reward yourself. Next time, set a slightly more challenging goal—try talking to a group of strangers. Then, set an even bigger goal. Reward yourself whether you succeed or not. Even if the strangers ignore you, you've accomplished your goal by reaching out.

Work your way up the ladder, taking slightly more significant risks each time until you've achieved your goals. If you want to talk to a stranger, start small. Read the room. Pick one person to talk to. Make eye contact with that person, then take the initiative.

If you have to, show them the pictures of your dog.

CHAPTER 44

Surviving as a Highly Sensitive Writer

There has been a lot of research into sensitivity recently. A research psychologist, Elaine Aron, wrote *The Highly Sensitive Person*. She writes that these people tend to be very empathic, intuitive, sensitive to sensory stimulation, and highly emotional.

A lot of writers fall into this category. They tend to process things more intensely. As a result, they can overreact. They have strong reactions to noises and busy, crowded places. They can have strong adverse reactions to being stuck in traffic.

These people also tend to be sensitive to emotional experiences. They catch shades of meaning others might not. A look could set them off. Highly sensitive people can easily become overwhelmed with emotionality.

Noisy, busy places, like shopping malls, can wreak havoc on their nerves. Packed schedules with high-pressure situations, like networking, will take their toll. If you feel you share this kind of high sensitivity, be careful you don't overdo it. Pace yourself.

On the weekends, take advantage of the days when you can sleep later and move at your own pace. Take plenty of breaks, treat yourself from time to time, and try not to be so hard on yourself.

Plan to decompress after a string of difficult situations. How do you decompress? Well, I happen to be an expert at decompressing. I can't count all the shows I've binge-watched on Netflix, Hulu, or Britbox.

Spend quality time with your spouse. Watch Netflix with your family. Find out what works for you. Go to dinner with a friend, see a movie, read a book, play with your dog, or get a massage. Get out of your head.

Create meaningful relationships

You're at your best when you're involved with someone who can relate to you at a deeper level. Lots of "lighter" relationships might not be right for you. A few more meaningful relationships will be important.

You're good at understanding what works for other people because of your empathy. Sensitive people tend to feel happy when they're helping others feel good. However, don't forget about yourself.

Develop healthy ways to manage conflict

You might find yourself feeling anxious when you deal with conflict. As a sensitive person, you tend to look at every question from both sides. You'll always see the other person's point of view. You'll struggle internally between getting what you think is right—and being nice.

Learn how to negotiate with others without arguing. Learn to discuss issues calmly. Be specific about what you want. Don't get caught up in name-calling or blaming. If you can, diffuse the situation with a joke.

Get plenty of sleep

Try to get at least seven hours of sleep. You'll want to give yourself a couple of hours to unwind before you go to sleep. Don't try to work right up to your bedtime. Don't exercise right up to your bedtime, either. I always break these rules and go to bed at 2 a.m.

Sensitive people need to find a relaxing activity before bedtime—like reading, listening to music, or watching TV. Without plenty of sleep, every little stressor will feel 10 times worse.

Be kind to yourself

Don't beat yourself up because you missed a meeting, got a rejection, or didn't place in a competition. Find a way to manage your expectations, slow your pace, and avoid overwhelming scenarios. Go easy on yourself, and challenge critical self-talk.

I recommend scheduling events and activities that you know you'll enjoy. Go to concerts, go out to movies with friends, go to the gym, swim in the ocean, go surfing, read books, play games, and watch TV.

Put some of these activities on your calendar. Always have something to look forward to. Writers spend so much time inside their heads—they need a break.

CHAPTER 45

Get Your Foot in the Door

You can break into screenwriting in a million different ways. Don't listen to people who tell you that you have to do it "their way." Like everything in this town, the only rule is there are no rules. You succeed in your own way.

You don't have to be laser-focused on a specific goal. Let's say you start out to write only one type of script, a period drama like *Gandhi* or *Judgment at Nuremberg*. Ask yourself, how many period dramas are studios making these days? How many of these screenplays are they buying from first-time writers?

Be open to writing other types of scripts. You have to think about screenwriting as a numbers game. Studios are more likely to buy horror films, thrillers, or comedies. Those types of films are cheaper to produce and generally have a broader appeal.

You'd be well advised to consider a broad range of possibilities. Take the opportunities that present themselves. The journey from where you are to where you want to be can be pretty circuitous. It's not a straight line.

Give yourself more ways to break in—don't limit yourself. If you tell yourself you'll never write a TV show, cartoon,

(God-forbid) reality show, documentary, or even a web series, you'll limit your chances at success.

Selling a low-budget film script or a TV episode will, hopefully, get you an agent. After you sign with an agent or manager and get your career on track, you can write that historical drama. When you write it, just know it will have to be one *kickass* script.

Whatever you write will have to blow people away. Agents don't like to send out "average" material. They have reputations, too. If they send out "just okay" screenplays, imagine what will happen. Producers will stop answering their phone calls. They'll be out of work.

Once you've got that foot in the door, you can't let up. There's no coasting in screenwriting. You need to keep doing your best work. Obvious, right? You'd be surprised. A lot of writers assume their agents will send out whatever they write. Not true.

Be willing to try new things.

Let's look at the way a few famous writers started out. James Brooks, for example, broke in writing documentaries. Brooks eventually won an Oscar for the screenplay for *Terms of Endearment*. Paul Haggis went from writing *One Day at a Time* to winning his Oscars for *Crash* and *Million Dollar Baby*.

Aaron Sorkin was a struggling playwright. John Ridley wrote for *The Fresh Prince of Bel-Air*. David O. Russell made a short called *Hairway to the Stars*. Jordan Peele wrote sketch comedy before writing the Oscar-winning horror film *Get Out*. He totally reinvented himself.

Animators Trey Parker and Matt Stone broke in with *South Park* and have since had success in features and on

Broadway. Larry David wrote jokes for *Fridays*. Bill Hader wrote for *Saturday Night Live*.

The point is, get your foot in the door, do good work, and get noticed. Whatever your strengths are, let people know about them, and always do your best work. Break in doing whatever clicks at first.

Still want to write that period drama?

So, they aren't very easy to sell right now. Should you stop writing them altogether? Of course not. I'm just suggesting you be open to writing a script with a high probability of selling. Low-budget horror. A Hallmark movie. A *Rick and Morty* episode.

No matter where you are in your career, the principle is the same. Don't limit yourself to one genre or format. The journey to success is rarely a straight line. You can do what James Brooks, Paul Haggis, and David O. Russell did—go from point A to points K, S, Y, and then Z.

Once again, it bears repeating—keep writing. Every successful writer will tell you that you have to persevere.

Next Steps

Now that you've read our guidelines for creating a successful screenwriting career, there are some next moves you might consider.

There are some other really good books out there that will help you with the nuts and bolts of screenwriting and TV writing. The thing is, there are so, so many.

I would recommend starting with two major books, *Save the Cat,* by Blake Snyder, and *Screenplay, The Foundations of Screenwriting,* by Syd Field. You can buy these books on Amazon using these links: amzn.to/40Y5rFm (*Save the Cat*) and amzn.to/3CAHMBA (*Screenplay*).

Every screenwriter should have those two books in their library. Other writers will disagree, and there are dozens of other excellent books to help you with what goes on the page. I would start with those two.

A few other great resources. Steve Cuden, a successful TV writer and co-creator of *Jekyll & Hyde, The Musical,* has written a great book called *Beating Hollywood.* He breaks down successful films into their story beats, which gives you a good idea of how to construct great stories. His book is available at amazon.to/42H2HgT.

Bob Saenz, a very successful screenwriter, (who works from Nashville, by the way) has a wonderful book called

That's Not The Way It Works, available on Amazon at *amzn.to/4hkJYfw*.

Another worthwhile addition to your library is William C. Martell's book, *Your Idea Machine*, also available on Amazon at https://shorturl.at/zjciH.

If you're interested in author, David Silverman's services for coverage or coaching check his site, HollywoodScriptwriting.com. If you're looking for a psychotherapist, check David's website at DavidSilvermanLMFT.com.

Essential Resources

There are a lot of great free online resources for writers, but there are so many it's hard to prioritize them. We've done that for you. Most of them offer free services. You can listen to free podcasts from screenwriters and screenwriting gurus like John Truby. You can also find ads for paid writing gigs. You can even download a huge library of great scripts for free.

*You can write screenplays on **Trelby** for free; just download it.*

1. Download, print, read, and "borrow" ideas from lots of great free screenplays online

You can Google "free screenplay downloads" and find tons of scripts to study. SimplyScripts.com is a great place to start. They have Oscar-nominated screenplays and TV shows. There's no substitute for reading great scripts when learning to write.

2. Download the best books ever written on screenwriting and read summaries for free

There are a million great books on screenwriting that you can buy on Amazon. However, let me save you some time and money.

You can read free useful summaries of *Save the Cat* and *Screenplay, The Foundations of Screenwriting*, and other great screenwriting books at www.bookey.app.

Erik Bork (*Band of Brothers*) has broken down the screenplay for *Legally Blonde* into the *Save The Cat* story beats at this free link: www.flyingwrestler.com/save-the-cat-beat-sheet/

Compare to the *Legally Blonde script:* www.dailyscript.com/scripts/legallblonde-shooting.pdf.

Best resources for free online networking
To build relationships with other writers, producers, agents, and directors, there are groups on LinkedIn, Facebook, and Meetup.com where you can make virtual friends and meet contacts face to face. Post on these sites, watch for activities, or set up coffee/drink meetings with like-minded creative professionals.

Groups on Meetup.com: Sunday Night Screenwriters Group, Ink Tank Screenwriter's Group, LA Actors and Filmmakers, Entertainment Entrepreneurs and Performers, Writers With Drinks (LA), LA Neo-Noir Cinemasters, and Creativity Workshop (LA).

Groups on LinkedIn: Film Angels, The Writer's Club of Los Angeles, and Film Job Board for Los Angeles. Stage 32. Film Financing Group, Film and TV Professionals, Independent Filmmakers.

Groups on Facebook: Screenwriting, Hippie-Dippie Hollywood Hopefuls, The Indie Film Scene, MOVIEWORLD, Get Reel!, The Craft of Screenwriting, Independent Film Society, Screenwriters Talking Shop, Cinema Discussions, Creative Designers and Writers, Film Industry Network, Writing in the Modern Age, Screenwriters Networking Group, Stage 32 Happy Writers. Don't forget to check out our Facebook group, How to Be A Rockstar Screenwriter (or at least pay the bills).

4. Read the best blogs and podcasts online for TV and screenwriters

I did a podcast with my friend, Steve Cuden. He has done hundreds of podcasts on his *StoryBeat* website. My favorite is Norman Steinberg (Blazing Saddles). Take a look. Mine can be found at: www.storybeat.net/david-silverman/.

International Screenwriters Association: All the podcasts they have are free to download. Besides myself, they have lots of great topics and interviews with screenwriting "gurus" like John Truby.

Read *Terry Rossio's Wordplay* (at wordplayer.com). He has 100s of "articles" on all aspects of screenwriting. He may be the highest-paid screenwriter in history, especially after the *Pirates of the Caribbean* franchise.

5. Post your screenplay, synopsis, or logline on a site that producers, filmmakers, and agents read

Inktip (inktip.com) is one of the first websites to post written material for industry professionals to find. It has some success stories. There is a monthly fee, but it's not a rip-off. It will also list your logline in a brochure sent to 5,000 production companies.

The Blacklist (blcklst.com) is one of the best newer services to offer this type of exposure. They charge $25 per month to post your material. They also offer evaluations of screenplays and TV scripts at reasonable prices and have contests and mentorship programs.

6. Online blasting services

Scriptblaster is a service that kind of replaces the need for an agent. Agents take 10%, so they're not free either. There is a charge for this service. They "blast" a copy of your screenplay and a query letter to hundreds of producers.

Unlike an agent, they won't give you feedback on your writing. For that, I recommend coverage services, screenwriting contests, or websites like The Blacklist or International Screenwriters Association.

Personal writing coaches also offer this type of feedback, as I do. I used to work in the Story Department, reading novels and scripts, summarizing them, and grading them for dialogue, story, character, etc. Ultimately, I would either check the PASS or RECOMMEND box.

7. Enter screenwriting contests to get your script out there

Moviebytes lists hundreds of screenwriting contests. The best three are Nicholls, Austin Film Festival, and Page. The Blacklist is up there, too. For independent films, I like the Slamdance Film Festival competition.

Before entering, make sure you get coverage from a reliable source; make sure the script gets a RECOMMEND evaluation. If it doesn't, rewrite it until it does. The Blacklist, Stage 32 Happy Writers, or HollywoodScriptwriting.com are good sources of coverage.

Believe it or not, several companies have developed Artificial Intelligence programs that read and offer coverage for your script. One of these services is Greenlight Coverage at glcoverage.com.

8. Take advantage of Personal Coaching

These days, nobody wants to risk having a script sent to agents or studios with flaws. You only get one chance to make a first impression on studio executives. Even professional, produced screenwriters want a second pair of eyes on their material before handing it in.

You want someone who's worked as a professional Story Analyst for a studio or production company to look at your script. Beyond the coverage, you may want to consult with a veteran screenwriter or TV writer. HollywoodScriptwriting.com offers great advice from me, a produced screenwriter and TV writer.

9. Coverage services that send out "Recommends" to producers

Some of the coverage services also offer to blast your finished script to hundreds of producers. Scriptshark, for example, provides this service. Of course, you want to ensure the script you send out gets a "Recommend," not a "Pass."

Spend more time having people read your screenplay before sending it out. Ask writer friends, people you know in studio Story Departments, or talent agencies to look at your script first. Keep improving it until you've collected a group of fans. Then, and only then, send it out.

10. Ways to get your finished script to producers if you don't have an agent

Some resources you can use to reach producers once your script is in great shape include Screenwriters Online, a website that will allow you to chat with a producer, and online pitch festivals like the one FadeIn Magazine (online) offers.

The International Screenwriting Association website advertises "Gigs." Most of these jobs are non-WGA writing jobs, so take advantage of them while you're working your way up and before you're in the guild. The producers advertising there will want to see a sample script of yours, preferably in the same genre.

IMDB and IMDB Pro are useful resources. A lot of the writers I know who are selling scripts, go to IMDB Pro to find producers who make the types of films they write. Then they send their scripts to those producers, along with a release form. You can download a release form for free at this link: https://bit.ly/4aLubEi.

Good luck and happy writing!

Acknowledgments

David Silverman

I would like to thank my amazingly talented writing partners over the years: Steven Sustarsic, Steve Pepoon, Howard Bendetson, Jack Carrerow, and Rogena Schuyler.

Additionally, I'd like to thank writer/producers Jay Moriarty, Lorenzo Music, Sam Locke, Ed Scharlack, and Tom Reeder, who were instrumental in the beginning of my career

I'd also like to thank Cindy Begel, Bob Bendetson, Diane Fraser, Russ Woody, Gary Miller, Robert Illes, and unforgettable bosses, including Brian Levant, Steven Spielberg, Larry Charles, Trey Parker, and Matt Stone for the career opportunities, for which I'll always be grateful. Special thanks to Vic Taybac at Alice for taking us all to the Santa Anita Racetrack to bet on his horses.

Thanks to Bill Walker, Jeffery Sherman, Joel Madison, Sid Youngers, Drew Carey, and Norm McDonald for the great times working together.

Thanks to the wonderful writers and friends from our days in development at Fox - Eric Shaw and Tim Schlattman.

I'd also like to take this opportunity to thank two of my biggest fans, my loving brother and sister, Rob Silverman and Lora Silverman Bronson.

Last but not least, thanks to the book's fantastic editor, Mary Rembert, our thoughtful beta reader, Mark Gunnion, and our publishing and marketing advisor, Geoff Affleck.

Rogena D. Schuyler

Undying love and gratitude to:

My grandmothers, Florence Norman and Mabel Schuyler, both teachers in the early 1900s. They both taught me the joy of reading and writing (having me write endless stories for them both). They encouraged me to pursue a career as a writer.

My mother, Faye Norman Schuyler, who always encouraged me to become a writer. Thanks for keeping and sharing everything I ever wrote.

My sister and best friend, Rhonda Schuyler Wages, for her constant support, encouragement, cheerleading, and laughter. You are my anchor.

My remarkable publishing mentors—Richard Singer, Morrie Mazur, Debbie Goffa, and Tina Antikadjian—who helped me become a better writer.

Additionally, a huge thanks to my good friends and editorial mavens, Ed Stockly and Chris Wolski, for their last minute editing solutions.

A huge thank you to my editorial production partner of many years, Cristina ˒ Paraiso Chavez, who kept me (relatively) sane.

And, of course, my sweet husband, partner, and co-author, David Silverman. Because…

About the Authors

David Silverman

David Silverman has co-created five TV series and has written for and/or produced more than 30 shows (for Robin Williams, ALF, Newhart, Tom Arnold, Rosanne, Drew Carey, Sarah Silverman, Pee Wee Herman, *Dilbert*, and *South Park*).

He co-created *The Wild Thornberrys* TV show, which spawned two feature films, including *Rugrats Go Wild*. Other feature films include *Stepping Out* for DeLaurentiis, *Purple Haze*, optioned by Caravan Pictures, and *The Flintstones Movie*, a Steven Spielberg production.

As a Stanford-educated psychotherapist, David has treated and coached aspiring writers, many of whom have since sold their own feature films and TV shows.

Contact David at HollywoodScriptWriter.com or DavidSilvermanLMFT.com.

Rogena D. Schuyler

Southern California-native Rogena D. Schuyler is a writer, editor, and screenwriter who has spent her life working on staff at several Los Angeles-based newspapers and periodicals, including *The Los Angeles Times*, *The Whittier*

Daily News, *This Week in Whittier*, *Orthopedic Technology Review*, and *Rehab Management*.

Additionally, she co-wrote and sold a TV pilot, *Bobcat*, and a feature-length screenplay, *Stepping Out*, to the DeLaurentiis Entertainment Group. Schuyler was also a writer on episodes of the animated NBC series *Spacecats*. She has been a member of the Writers Guild of America since 1987.

Schuyler is currently working on the "Great American Novel."

Did you enjoy this book?

Your feedback helps us provide the best quality books and helps other readers like you.

It would mean the world to us if you took two minutes to share your thoughts about the book as a book review.

Post your review here: https://amzn.to/4jSkoQ2

www.ingramcontent.com/pod-product-compliance
Lightning Source LLC
Chambersburg PA
CBHW020539030426
42337CB00013B/905